# FINDING GOD

## The Real Thing

## Paul Weimer

# ACKNOWLEDGEMENTS

With deep appreciation and many thanks to those
who have contributed to and helped so much
in preparing this manuscript with welcome advice,
editing and typing.
Thank you Cathy Muth, Rebecca Hibpshman, and Ladonna
Lindley.
May your loving work help to lead others in the Way,
the Truth, and the Life.

# CONTENTS

# FOREWORD

*F*inding God. Is the title a contradiction? A man might say, "I did not find God; He found me. I was the one who was lost. God was not lost." That is pleasantly true. Furthermore, mankind does not naturally seek God in truth. "There is none that seeketh after God" (Romans 3:11). When God came looking for Adam, estranged by sin, the man ran away and tried to hide from his Maker. We have been doing that ever since.

Yet, in another sense, wherever we travel in this world, we find people searching for something. A thousand religious cults and beliefs bear witness to the hunt. Often, these cults and beliefs contradict each other in tenets and doctrines, resulting in massive confusion. The Apostle Paul wrote of those who "have a zeal for God, but not according to knowledge."

Another evidence of the search is the despondency and empti-ness of soul that leads so many to despair, and often suicide, which sadly ranks near the top causes of death. Psychologists' offices are busy. Often, the despondent one cannot figure out the reason for the emptiness within; he turns to drugs, booze, or wild partying to satisfy the gnawing. In doing so he gets on a merry-go-round with a worse let-down at the end of the ride.

It is as if a man knows he lost a treasure in Alaska, so he goes looking all over Arizona to find it. He does not search in the right place. The Bible describes some as, "Ever learning, and never able to come to the knowledge of the truth" (II Timothy 3:7).

An increasingly popular suggestion is that we should just forget our differences, accept everybody's ideas, and compromise our own. They say there can be no absolutes of truth or morality. We just keep searching. How long? Forever? If there are no answers in the absolute, why bother? To say that everybody is right will not do. It is illogical to say that two opposing propositions are both true. It cannot be, for truth is never illogical. If one proposition is true, its opposite cannot be true. It is supremely important to find the real and the true. The life of the soul depends upon it.

There is a narrow gate leading to the abundant life. It is possible to "...understand the fear of the Lord, and find the knowledge of God" (Proverbs 2:5). The dividend is happiness and peace. "He is a rewarder of them that diligently seek Him" (Hebrews 11:6). "Blessed (happy) are they that keep His testimonies, and that seek Him with the whole heart" (Psalm 119:2).

'Twas the greatest of all discoveries when I found Jesus my Lord.

# CHAPTER 1

# REAL GOOD

"The Lord is…" Without a doubt, there are a million ways to finish that sentence. Perhaps the best is the simple, heartwarming statement, "The Lord is good." It is constantly repeated throughout the Bible – about 20 times in the Psalms alone. "The Lord is good to all…" (Psalm 145:9). To anyone who calls upon Him in truth, He is good. Could anyone imagine otherwise, that God is not good? Impossible, for goodness comes from and goes with God. "For the Lord is good…" (Psalm 100:5). He is always good, and I would emphasize *always*. There can *never* be a time, a place, or an occasion where He is not good.

But then, in speaking of His goodness to all, it is possible to be rather impersonal about it. The "me" gets lost in the crowd of "us". Great comfort and strength belong to the one who learns that personal relationship, that closeness in the possessive "me". The Lord is *my* God; therefore, His goodness is to me. If that is not so, then the goodness of God is no more than a cold, impersonal dogma, of no practical value to me. The local bank may be full of assets, but if none of them are mine, it may as well not exist for it does not help me.

What is it that the Lord is good? Goodness is understood to be excellence in morals, in virtue, in character. It is generous, kind, and helpful. Even a toddler likes to be called "good boy" or "good girl". And yet, how we struggle with it. The little boy tries to be a good boy, but sometimes he is not, in spite of himself. More than one good boy has grown up to become a rogue. As adults, we do pretty well at being good to ourselves. And sometimes, if we are good to others, our appetite for praise spoils the action. Self-focus hinders goodness.

Where did the good idea of goodness come from? And where is it found? As with everything else the craftsman does, the building of goodness needs two things: first, a pattern, second, the power of performance. The idea or principle of goodness, of course, comes from God. It is *His* goodness. It comes from Him (Psalm 107:8, 15, 21, 31). He has given to us the pattern for goodness, and also makes available to us the power and the ability to perform. Both pattern and power are in Christ our Savior. God in Christ is perfect goodness. He is the pattern. Christ living in the believer is the dynamic and the power to goodness.

As long as God exists (and that is a long, long time), He must always be good. His goodness is the transmission of His love. Illustrations are everywhere. Ravens, eagles, and sparrows are fed. Roses, daisies and tulips are painted in all different hues. Grass in the field is clothed (Luke 12: 24, 27, 28). The rainbow, the sunrise, the return of the seasons, and the very air we breathe all testify to the goodness of God.

Sometimes we think we see evidence to the contrary. Maybe God is not always good? A loved one gets desperately ill, or a winsome young life is snuffed out and the question lurks, "If God is good, why does He permit misery, war, and heartache?" The answer, at least in part, must be that God is not the author of bad things. When He had finished His creation, He looked at it all and said it was all very good, including Adam! (Genesis 1:31).

Then came Satan and introduced sin into the picture. Sin means to turn aside, to come short, to rebel, to transgress. "Wherefore, as by one man sin entered into the world, and death by sin, and so death passed upon all men, for all have sinned" (Romans 5:12). It is the result of that, which is so painfully obvious: Where goodness is absent, sin is present.

Another part of the answer is found in this: Our all-wise and sovereign God has, without a doubt, some long-range plans that stretch across the years of this life and even beyond. It may seem impossible when we are hurting that He could bring good out of the hurt, but He is infinite in His power, His foresight, and His wisdom as well as sovereign in control. He is goodness absolutely; therefore, He cannot do wrong. Ever. When He says, "All things work together for good to them that love God..." (Romans 8:28), He means it. "All things" covers all things.

# CHAPTER 2

# THE REAL ME

Fundamental to finding God is finding one's self. We do not search for something unless we need it. What am I? What is lacking? We tend to focus on the appearance and the actions of the physical body. But the reflection in the mirror does not show the real self. A body is not all there is to our person – or even the most important part of "me". There is a motivator, a director, and a pilot that directs the body.

The body is the tool of the soul. If the body does badly, it is because the soul is bad. Hopefully we do not all do bad things all the time, but, truth is, we all do bad things, or say bad things, at least some of the time. The body sins because there is sin in the soul. A diseased apple tree will not produce great apples. Jesus said, "…neither can a corrupt tree bring forth good fruit" (Matthew 7:18).

For example, we hate a lie. We do not trust the liar. However, if the issue is financial profit or loss, or protecting ourselves, we are tempted to shave the truth a bit. My grandfather was honest, and shrewd in business. As a mail carrier, he clocked a lot of miles on his car. He kept the vehicle in immaculate condition. At the time of the sale, the purchaser wondered how a car of that vintage could show such low mileage, and be in such fine condition. He asked my grandfather, "Is that the original mileage?" Grandfather answered, "Yes," but he did not say that the odometer had rolled over long before. I can still see my grandfather's grin as he related the deal.

The Bible's assessment says, "The heart is deceitful above all things, and desperately wicked; who can know it?" (Jeremiah 17:9). It is natural for us to think we are good, perhaps even better than average.

Hazael was an officer of the King of Syria. One day, Elisha the prophet met him and predicted that he would commit terrible atrocities and murders. Hazael protested vigorously. "Me? Am I a dog? Why, I would never do such things!" But he did. The story is recorded in II Kings 8.

The Apostle Paul was wiser when he wrote, "I know that in me, [that is, in my flesh] dwelleth no good thing_" (Romans 7:18). Of course, if evolution is right, we are but animals, so there are no moral absolutes, and no such thing as sin or a sinful soul.

I was amused as I watched a television news anchor interview a so-called scientist. He was simply elated that a monkey had been taught to jab some numbers to get something to eat. Eureka! The monkey had mathematical abilities! I smiled, because we had previously visited Knott's Berry Farm where a Rhode Island Red Hen sang in her little cage. Following directions, I put a quarter in a slot and watched that hen go over to a little toy piano, and with her beak play "Mary Had A Little Lamb". Does that make a chicken a musician? To what unreasonable extremes will we go to try to prove we are related to monkeys?

The last thing we want to admit is that we have a sinful soul that results in sinful actions and speech. It is our great embarrassment. The body sins because the heart is sinful. "For out of the abundance of the heart the mouth speaketh" (Matthew 12:34). "For as (a man) thinketh in his heart, so is he" (Proverbs 23:7). "_For out of (the heart) are the issues of life" (Proverbs 4:23).

The religious zealots of Jesus' day thought they could please God by the constant practice of outer religious acts. Jesus changed the focus. He taught that the heart must first be made right. It was a dramatic change of emphasis from the outer, bodily action to the condition of the inner and real self. Not that outer practice of religion should be abandoned. Speaking of tithing (religious practice) He said, "…these ought ye to have done, and not to leave the other undone" (Luke 11:42).

We would not say that mankind is incapable of doing some good things with the body. Family love and care, charitable giving, helping those who are weak or sick – these and more are commendable. Bad men sometimes do well, whether by accident or by intention. Some of the image of God, though marred, is still present, even in evil men. Yet, whatever good there may be is tainted! "_all our righteousnesses are as filthy rags_" (Isaiah 64:6). The awful truth stands. "For there is not a just man upon earth, that doeth good and sinneth not" (Ecclesiastes 7:20). We will deal more with this in a later chapter.

Why do people die? Science cannot give an answer, but the Bible does. "…the soul that sinneth, it shall die" (Ezekiel 18:4). "As by one man sin entered into the world, and death by sin, and so death passed upon all men, for all have sinned" (Romans 5:12).

If we are going to find peace with God, we must agree with God. We must confess our need to ourselves and to Him and our desire for His gift of redemption in the new birth, which is a radical makeover of the soul. "Except a man be born again, he cannot see the kingdom of God" (John 3:3).

No philosophy, no ethic, no politic, no pursuit can match the importance of finding God and real life.

# CHAPTER 3

# THE REAL GOD

In *"Finding God,"* it is assumed (and a well-substantiated truth) that He *is*. "The Lord is," and I repeat, there are a million ways to complete that sentence. The first truth, however, is this: God is.

I read about a little bug that started from ground level, worked and struggled until it finally reached the top of the horse's ear, from which it could view the horse's head. It then congratulated itself for such an awesome achievement in its amazing universe, never dreaming that there was far more to the horse. Ego-centered people are like that. Miniature accomplishments swell miniature heads until we assume we are the reason and end of the universe.

Then one day we look again. We begin to see the complex order, power, and beauty that amaze us. Every effect must have been caused, and not one of these observed effects can be as great, or greater than their cause.

That well-performing horse must have had a trainer. Who taught the goose, the arctic tern, or the monarch butterfly to make their incredible journeys? Where did the laws of gravity and magnetism come from? Rain falls, water freezes and thaws, and airplanes fly because there are fixed and dependable laws. Who engineered the hydrologic cycle of vapor suspended, to rain, to river, to ocean, and back to vapor? It was mentioned 3000 years ago in Ecclesiastes 1:7 and again in Jeremiah 10:13.

Who fashioned the eye that can read or send a message with a glance? Man's best attempts at photography cannot match it. Could the camera make itself? Who designed the brain? We might think that some brains were accidents, but they were not. No man-made computer can compare to the brain. And where did the spirit-mind come from that feeds the computer brain? How wonderful are the air, oxygen, lungs, and blood arrangement, so vital to sustain our existence.

Why does a tree gather nutrients from the soil, carry them upward (in spite of gravity), through its own transportation system, combine them with products of its leaf factories, and so sustain itself? Did the tree figure that out by itself?

"The heavens declare the glory of God, and the firmament showeth His handiwork. Day unto day uttereth speech, and night unto night showeth knowledge. There is no speech nor language where their voice is not heard" (Psalm 19:1-3). Even a casual consideration of these things points to intelligent design and performance power. A thousand examples could be added. Why then, this reluctance to look to God? Surely intelligence recognizes intelligence.

People often speak of the power and beauty of nature. Terrific winds, destructive storms, hurricanes, and earthquakes all cause us to watch in awe. I have often heard men speak of the power of Mother Nature. I want to ask, "Who is she? Please introduce me."

Others talk about Mother Earth. Mother Earth never had any children. Perhaps ascribing a personality to the inanimate earth is just a figure of speech. More probably, it exposes a reluctance to vocalize a belief in a personal, sovereign God who "(upholds) all things by the word of His power" (Hebrews 1:3). There is a reason for that reluctance.

Not long ago, following a big earthquake, a television news anchor claimed that Mother Earth is finally getting angry at all the environmental abuse and pollution we humans have piled on her, and through the earthquake was saying, "Enough!" "She" is capable of anger and rational speech?

But no one said a word about God's part in it all. Why, to attribute such things to a personal Creator God would give them apoplexy for sure! Having forsaken the Bible Truth of the Great

Sovereign who governs the universe, it is easy to give intellect and power to a non-existent, fuzzy something or other called Mother Earth or Mother Nature. Of course, it is okay to talk about "divine intervention" as a joke to explain a win in an athletic contest.

For the record, the Lord is the one who can shake the world. "_I will shake the heavens, and the earth, and the sea, and the dry land; and I will shake all nations, and the desire of all nations shall come…" (Haggai 2:6-7). He said, "Yet once more I shake not the earth only, but also heaven." And this word, "Yet once more, signifieth the removing of those things that are shaken…" (Hebrews 12:26-27). We would be wise to consider that natural catastrophes may be the voice of God trying to get our attention. Our generation speaks of values, then thumbs its nose at God, breaking His rules, and laughing all the way to the judgment.

Animism is a form of religious idolatry descended to us from primitive times. It is a belief that nature, animals, birds, trees, et cetera possess some sort of wispy, indefinable force of intelligence that gives order, planning, and reproduction. It is to "exchange the truth of God for a lie, and worship and serve the creature more than the Creator, who is blessed forever" (Romans 1:25) because "_they did not like to retain God in their knowledge_" (Romans 1:28).

God is. God forever will be. He is not a "what" but a "who". When everything is all said, done, and over, we must all give an accounting to God, who *is*.

By definition, God is exclusive. That is, He only and He alone is God. There is none other. "_there is no other God but one. For though there be that are called gods… to us there is but one God the Father, of whom are all things, and we in Him; and one Lord Jesus Christ, by whom are all things, and we by Him" (I Corinthians 8:4-6). "Hear, O Israel: the Lord our God is one Lord" (Deuteronomy 6:4). "…before me there was no god formed, neither shall there be after me" (Isaiah 43:10). All other so-called gods are simply not gods. They are false gods, idols, by whatever name. Of logical necessity, God must be God alone.

By definition God is sovereign, sovereign over all, even mankind! He must be in total control of all things. If a single thing or event is not under His control, He ceases to be God. He "worketh all things after the counsel of His own will" (Ephesians 1:11). Suppose that tomorrow a storm catches God off guard, so that He does not know about it, or control it. One event like that could trigger another, and then another and another until everything would be an accident. We need our sleep. God does not. "He who keepeth Israel shall neither slumber nor sleep" (Psalm 121:4). There is wonderful order in God's universe because He is absolutely sovereign.

By definition God is faithful. "…He abideth faithful; He cannot deny Himself" (II Timothy 2:13). He always finishes whatever He starts. And He always carries out His own word, fulfilling His own predictions. When He says that something is going to happen, while it may be yet future in our timeline, it is as certain as though it were history. When He gives eternal life to the person who trusts Christ, that life cannot end because God is faithful. Eternal is eternal. The true Christian is confidently assured that, "He who hath begun a good work in you will perform it until the day of Jesus Christ" (Philippians 1:6).

While there is much more that we do know about God, such as His love, wisdom, power, and beauty, we obviously cannot know all there is to know. Every imaginable superlative has been used, but He is beyond human language and thought. No horizon is big enough to contain Him. That is one reason why He forbids our making an image of Him. In our feeble attempts to describe Him, we should not be so foolishly presumptuous as to think that we can come close. The infinite is without limits. As mere created beings, time, space, and matter strictly limit us. The Creator is not limited. To illustrate, consider something Jesus said of Himself, "No man hath ascended up to heaven, but he that came down from heaven, even the Son of Man who is in heaven" (John 3:13). That was a remarkable statement, for He was at that moment standing before Nicodemus. The only way it could be true was for Jesus to be unlimited and present in two places at the same time – omnipresent. His home was in heaven; yet, He was here and could move from one sphere to another at will. Moses said, "The secret things belong unto the Lord our God; but those things which are revealed belong unto us…" (Deuteronomy 29:29).

So, all we know for sure about God and how to approach Him are those things He has shown us, either in His wonderful creation or in His wonderful word. That is more than enough to incline us to investigate. I am reminded of what the Apostle John wrote after he had done his best in describing our Lord, "There are also many other things which Jesus did, which, if they should be written every one, I suppose that even the world itself could not contain the books that should be written" (John 21:25). Our limited understanding should fill the heart and mind with wonder, motivating us to seek Him. Aren't you glad that there is Someone there who is greater, and dearer than all? "And ye shall seek me, and find me, when ye shall search for me with all your heart" (Jeremiah 29:13).

When questioned about God, the Bible, the origin of life, or the right road to heaven, men often respond with, "I do not know," or something similar. People can talk intelligently about sports, politics, investments – any subject but the most important. In fact, sometimes they seem to think it is a virtue to be illiterate about God. Perhaps it reveals a poorly hidden prejudice. By nature, we run away from God, like Adam, after his sin. Rebels; a self-made enemy. That is God's assessment of the natural man. Man really does not want to know.

II Peter 3 speaks of a willful ignorance. As soon as we admit to ourselves God *is*, we logically must admit to a responsibility to Him as sovereign and our Creator. And when we see that Christ died for us and then rose from the dead, we must also see that we need to do something about that.

The Lord is. There is ample and convincing proof everywhere. The beauty, order, precision in nature, our bodies, our computer brains – everything shouts it loud and clear. "Since the creation of the world, His invisible attributes, His eternal power and divine nature, have been clearly seen, being understood through what has been made, so that they are without excuse" (Romans 1:20 New American Standard Bible).

The real and burning issue for us is not does God exist, or is the Bible true, or is the Christian faith valid for the 21st century. Of course, it is. The question is, do I want to know? What am I doing with what I already know?

Personal freedom. Independence. Self-esteem. Democracy. These concepts are enjoyed in our great land more than in any other country. But the treasured specialties of American life often become contributors to personal conflict and too many emotional and spiritual catastrophes.

"No one can tell me what to do" declares an attitude that has landed many couples in divorce court and teenagers in jail. Doesn't a parent have the inherent right to expect obedience from the child to whom he has given life and nurture? Doesn't an employer who built his business have the right to make some rules and receive respect?

We have made pride a virtue and humility a vice. We have trouble even defining a Christian grace like meekness. We expect and demand honor and good treatment from others while we do poorly in giving it. We insist on having our own way. We cannot admit to having done wrong, even when that wrong is obvious.

Just a few years ago there was a popular song, "I Did It My Way". Can you imagine saying that to the sovereign God? That is the sin that changed Lucifer into Satan and expelled him from heaven. Only one single tree in all God's Garden of Eden was forbidden fruit, but Satan whispered, "Don't let God tell you what to do. It's desired to make you wise" (Genesis 3:5-6). Self-interest can become so prominent in our thinking that everyone else, including God, is crowded out.

Personal freedom is wonderful. Left untempered by submission to our Creator and His moral government, virtue, and righteous action, it becomes both a social and a personal destroyer. When we, as a society, stopped believing in God and promoted believing in self and gratifying self-appetites, we lost a moral foundation. Violence and greed grow like weeds when freedom becomes license. It is past time to surrender and submit to God. It is impossible to "find" God until we come to that crisis point.

# CHAPTER 4

# THE REAL GOD-MAN

In pursuing the subject of finding God, we have to consider Jesus, the Son of God. The often-repeated claim throughout the Bible is that Jesus is the one and only door to God. "There is one God and one mediator between God and men, the man, Christ Jesus" (I Timothy 2:5). He said, "...no man cometh to the Father but by me" (John 14:6). What a daring statement! A rational person would not say that unless it were true. Every investigator must decide whether Jesus spoke with shameless audacity, or was He speaking perfect truth? Those who have entered the gate to life know.

The essential deity of Christ and the only way of salvation are stated in the very plainest of terms. So plain in fact that we can read it, as one said, on the run. And yet there is no subject about which more falsehood and error has been preached or written. I have heard men say that Jesus never claimed to be God. Can't they read? So opposed are men to the gospel that their eyes cannot see what they read. The easiest words are twisted and distorted. "The god of this world hath blinded the minds of them that believe not" (II Corinthians 4:4).

Who was Jesus of Nazareth? That is the question. Does He remain a question mark, or is He indeed the exclamation point of history? When He was only a boy of 12 years, He confounded the educated temple leaders with His understanding (Luke 2:47). Later, His contemporaries who witnessed His amazing miracles asked,

"Who do you claim to be?" (John 8:25). At His final trial, the puzzled governor, Pilate, questioned Him about His identity. Jesus asked His disciples, "Who do men say that I, the Son of man, am?" (Matthew 16:13). Serious people, religious or not, are still faced with the puzzle. The answer we give is important with consequences that last forever.

Consider the claims. Jesus accepted John's witness that He was the declaration of God (John 1:18). He said that He was equal with The Father God, "I and my Father are one" (John 10:30). He said that even the great Abraham who had lived 2000 years before saw Him (John 8:56). He said He was the great self-existing "I AM" (John 8:58). He accepted the worship due only to God (John 20:28). He said He saw Satan cast out of heaven. He said that all the Old Testament scriptures testified of Him (John 5:39, Luke 24:27). He claimed only what God could claim, that is, He had all authority in heaven and earth (Matthew 28:18). When His opposers attempted to execute Him by stoning, the reason they gave was that He blasphemed by making Himself God (John 10:33), a capital crime then – and the only valid accusation they could make as cause to crucify Him (Matthew 26:63-66).

If all the things Jesus Christ said about Himself are true, then He is the exclamation point of history. The record of His perfection as well as His miracles demonstrates that truth. On the other hand, if they are not true, then He is a riddle without integrity, for He led multitudes to believe that He was God come in human flesh. Now, I have met a lot of people who have not yet surrendered to Him, but I do not recall any who dared call Him a liar. Unthinkable, for His credibility and integrity are established beyond question. He is truth. He always did (and does) what He said He would do, even rising from the dead.

Names of many famous people are sprinkled throughout human history. Men and women have gained renown through exploits of various sorts. No story of any other human life comes close to the wonder of Jesus Christ. The Son of God stands unique, alone, and supreme. Examine all the best and we soon find out that there is none other like Him. His is obviously a divine story. No human author could invent such a story as His. In more ways than one, history is, indeed, His story.

God, Creator of heaven and earth, took on Himself the form of His created. So much did He love fallen humanity that He purposed to become one of them. The timeless one entered time in human flesh to experience our condition, sin excepted, so that He could act as our substitute, the surrogate sufferer, the sinless Son of God, paying in full the sin debt of all who would receive Him.

Can anyone imagine or explain the infinite God becoming an infant, born in a stable? Dependent on His mother? Obedient to a human father? Learning the carpenter's trade? Speaking incomparable words? Giving sight to the hopelessly blind? Commanding and controlling stormy seas and wind? There was the absolutely guiltless man, voluntarily submitting Himself to the accusations and insults of hypocrites. And there was the final proof of His identity and total authority over everything: His bodily resurrection.

A lot of material has been published about so-called "out-of-body-experiences." They all fall short of proving anything. They add to fanciful speculations about life after death that are of little profit. However, there is one who actually came back from the grave after having been certified dead. "I am He that liveth, and was dead; and, behold, I am alive forevermore, Amen, and have the keys of hell and of death" (Revelation 1:18). The Lord Jesus Christ rose physically from the dead after being sealed in a tomb for three days. If that happened today, the media would be filled with the incredibly exciting story.

One man claimed exultantly, "We can create life in our lab!" I told him he was lying, for if he could, he would be the hero of the world and its richest man.

We have trouble even defining life, much less creating or hanging onto it. Consider these various definitions of life from the dictionary: "The period of an individual's existence between birth and death, " or "The characteristic state or condition of an organism that has not died".

Life is God's property. Jesus said, "For as the Father has life in Himself, so hath He given to the Son to have life in Himself" (John 5:26). Concerning the Son, John wrote, "In Him was life; and the life was the light of men" (John 1:4). His resurrection is proof.

# CHAPTER 5

# REAL LIFE

Finding God is inseparably linked to finding life. Get rightly connected to God and we have life. The common notion about how to come to God and make that vital connection is that it does not make much, if any, difference, how we approach, as long as we come. The method is a matter of personal choice. Each in his own way. There are those who think that we should never try to persuade another as to the right way. But, if I see you walking toward a death trap, I have a moral responsibility to warn you.

It is possible to try to do a good thing in a wrong way, and so ruin or nullify the effort. In coming to God, the result is forever.

True worship of God is a matter of divine revelation, not human invention. It is not the conclusion drawn from a symposium. It is not like a table at a crafts sale to display every person's differing tastes. Rather, it is a plan fixed and framed by God, Himself. He is the One who can dictate how His creatures come to Him. Otherwise we would be like little children crying in the dark for a father we could not find. The child who walks in the clear footsteps of a loving father will not make a mistake.

"…The Father sent the Son to be the Savior of the world" (I John 4:14). Suppose I am a traveler in a strange country and lose my way. I go to a native of that country and ask directions. When he points out the right way to me, I would be foolish to disregard his directions and choose a way that appeals to me. No telling where I might end up. God's Word is that Jesus is the way to life and God. "I am the way, the truth, and the life; no man cometh unto the Father but by me" (John 14:6). To disregard Christ or attempt another way to God is to question God, Himself, and endanger myself.

Jesus said, "I am the door; by me if any man enter in, he shall be saved..." (John 10:9). Doors. If we are going to have a door, we want it to work right, opening when we want it to open, and staying closed when we want it closed, and opening to the right place. A door functions to let me in my house and provide security. It also keeps out the undesirables – like minus 20-degree temperatures!

We had a church building with seven outside doors – I guess to be certain no one got stuck in church – of all places! The Bible has a lot to say about doors. "As the door turneth upon its hinges, so doth the slothful upon his bed" (Proverbs 26:14). That is an interesting picture! "...narrow is the gate (door), and hard is the way, which leadeth unto life, and few there be that find it" (Matthew 7:14). The door to heaven is narrow and single. Many who assume they will enter will be shut out forever. Jesus said that He is that door (John 10:9). Further, He said that He is the only door there. "I am the way (door) ...no man cometh unto the Father, but by me" (John 14:6). Then, there is the door to our hearts. We are the only ones who control that door. We can open it, or close it. He knocks on that door, seeking to enter there with all His blessings and everlasting life (Revelation 3:20).

Faith in Christ is also likened to a good and reliable foundation. My family and I once lived in a house in Alaska with a failing, crumbling foundation. The cement block wall that once looked so nice, and the concrete floor slab just went all to pieces. The place was less than four years old, but the builder, recently up from the South, had built on clay – clay mud with little steel for reinforcing. Hard frosts of three cold winters soon destroyed it. We had to move the house.

Pay attention to the foundation. Whether building a family, a church, or your own individual life, make sure the foundation is built on the Lord Jesus Christ. Any other footing will not endure in the day when "the fire shall try every man's work of what sort it is" (I Corinthians 3:13).

There are three important considerations as we examine this foundation. First, who is Christ? A lot of so-called Christian institutions deny the essential nature of the Savior, Jesus Christ. They deceptively use and claim His holy name, but upon examination, define Him differently. You can have a Christ who is not the Biblical Christ. The real one is the Creator of all things and therefore, Lord of all. He laid the foundation of the earth, and the heavens are the work of His hands (Hebrews 1:10).

Second, what this Christ has done to rescue us must be part of the foundation. He was foreordained to redeem us from our sins with His own blood from the foundation of the world (I Peter 1:18-20). "Without the shedding of blood there is no remission" (Hebrews 9:22). The saving work of the Son of God on the old rugged cross was, from the beginning, a part of the Architect's plan.

Third, the words of Christ need to be in our foundation. The Word of God is essential to our enduring structure. "Whosoever heareth these sayings of mine, and doeth them, I will liken him unto a wise man, who built his house upon a rock" (Matthew 7:24). When the storms and wind came (they will), it did not fall. Jesus is this true foundation, both sure and eternal. "For other foundation can no man lay than that which is laid, which is Jesus Christ" (I Corinthians 3:11). Check your foundation. You cannot afford not to!

So, who is Christ? What part should He have in our lives? The answer we give is supremely important. Nearly everyone agrees about Him – up to a point. All agree that He was an outstanding, good, unusual, helpful person in history. Healer, philosopher, example – He was all of that. No one can seriously argue against those points.

But the fact is, as previously noted, He claimed to be far more. Consider these statements: "I and my Father are one." "He that hath seen me hath seen the Father." When doubting Thomas called Him "my Lord and my God," Jesus did not correct him, but rather commended him. The Apostle Paul wrote, "...all things were created by Him, and for Him" (Colossians 1:16b), and, "For in Him dwelleth all the fullness of the Godhead bodily" (Colossians 2:9). There is much more as the Bible clearly and repeatedly declares the essential and unique deity of Jesus, the Christ.

"...God sent forth His Son, made of a woman..." (Galatians 4:4). "Sent forth" demands that the Son of God existed as the Eternal Son before Bethlehem. He said, "Before Abraham was, I am." He had neither beginning of days nor end of life (Hebrews 7:3).

If it should ever turn out that He was (or is) something less than one with the eternal God, then the whole gospel message is nothing but a great hoax. But then, there was His resurrection from the dead, the final demonstration.

The resurrection of Jesus is the foundation of Christianity. That is why God saw to it that it should be so firmly documented. The risen Christ showed Himself physically alive after his certified death "by many infallible proofs" (Acts 1:3). Here are some of those proofs.

There is the empty tomb. That is the proof that caused His disciple, John, to believe (John 20:8-9). Both the Jews and the Romans would have given anything if someone could only produce the corpse and thus stop the spreading flame of Christianity, but that dead body was living again and beyond their reach.

Then, there is the record of at least ten appearances of the risen Savior to one or to a group of people. Some of these are listed in I Corinthians 15. They were not hallucinations, or the effect of mob psychology, or "ghosts" for He had "flesh and bones" (Luke 24:39). They actually touched Him (1 John 1:1). They talked to Him. They heard Him speak. They ate with Him. Furthermore, they had not expected Him to be alive, for they simply did not believe His often-repeated predictions of His resurrection (John 20:9).

There is also the powerful witness of the complete and total commitment of His followers. Those infallible proofs so convinced His disciples and a multitude of others that they transformed their lives. They were willing to live and to die to support and defend the truth. They often suffered the loss of all personal property, torture, and execution. They had every incentive to deny His resurrection; yet, not one recanted, often choosing martyrdom rather than to deny the risen Savior.

The question of the Apostle Paul to King Agrippa was, "Why should it be thought a thing incredible with you that God should raise the dead?" (Acts 26:8). Since God is God, the infinite posses-sor, origin, and giver of life, and since He must be omnipotent, certainly He could raise to life one who was dead.

And this word as it relates to our eternal salvation: The resurrec-tion of Jesus demonstrated the wonderful fact that the absolute justice of God in heaven was satisfied with His substitutionary sacrifice on the cross. "(He) was delivered for [on account of] our offenses, and was raised again for [on account of] our justification" (Romans 4:25).

# CHAPTER 6

# REAL LIGHT

O nce I encountered a man who hated churches and preachers. He was vocal about it! Among his bitter accusations was that Christianity has been the cause of all wars! Of course, that is not even close to true. Religion maybe, but true faith in Jesus Christ has never caused a war. What it does cause is peace. Wherever He is believed and followed, the effect is always good. There are a lot of pseudonyms for Christianity and a lot of false Christs. I speak of the person of the Bible. No person in history, no ethic, no philosophy has had such a great and good influence on our world.

He is the Light of the World. "…he that followeth me shall not walk in darkness, but shall have the light of life" (John 8:12). He is called, "the Sun of righteousness" (Malachi 4:2). John wrote, "In Him was life; and the life was the light of men" (John 1:4). "God is light, and in Him is no darkness at all" (I John 1:5). The Sun of God's goodness and righteousness shines across this world in the person of His Son. When we receive Christ by faith, the Light of Life comes in and turns on the light. "The Lord is my light…" (Psalm 27:1).

The alternative, the opposite, is evil, wickedness, unrighteousness, and sin. These are always associated with darkness. Interestingly, greed is said to be the foundation of evil. "The love of money is a root of all sorts of evil" (I Timothy 6:10 New American Standard Bible). Note it is not money that is evil. Money is only matter, and matter is not a moral agent. It is the love of money – the insatiable appetite for it

– that is the dark producer of evil. We see proof of that statement everywhere. The alcohol dispenser excuses himself and keeps on contributing to the life-destroying scourge for the love of money. The pornography peddler promotes his dark message for money. Prostitution exists for money. The abortionist works for money. TV producers put out their envelope-pushing trash for money. The traitor sells his country's secrets for money. Gamblers think betting will provide money to help pay their bills. The thought is that if immorality, violence, and playing to man's basest nature produce financial profit, then it must be all right. Motivated by the love of money, the light grows dim and the world sinks in darkness. "Woe unto them who call evil, good, and good, evil; who put darkness for light, and light for darkness..." (Isaiah 5:20).

What is morally wrong cannot be economically right. "Ye cannot serve God and money" (Matthew 6:24). You cannot serve two masters. Three statements from the Book of Psalms lead in the right direction. "Thy word is a lamp unto my feet, and a light unto my path" (Psalm 119:105). "The entrance of thy words giveth light..." (Psalm 119:130). "Thy word have I hidden in mine heart, that I might not sin against thee" (Psalm 119:11).

The Christ of the Bible is still the Light of the World. When a man or a woman, tired of the darkness, turns in faith to trust the crucified, risen Lord, there is a new birth. We are "delivered from the power of darkness, and translated... into the kingdom of His dear Son" (Colossians 1:13).

Suppose that Jesus had not come into our world. There would be:

1. No Christian churches where multitudes sing of Him and where standards of right and wrong are declared. Salt of the earth.
2. No great universities as Cambridge, Harvard, and Yale, for they originated as training schools for Christian pastors.
3. No America as we know it, for our nation's founders believed in Christ and came here for freedom of worship.
4. No hospitals, for they were started because of Christian benevolence.

5. No Christian marriages or true "family values".
6. No agape love, for that brand of selfless, giving, sacrificing love was unknown to the world before Jesus Christ came (See I John 4:9).
7. No moral standards as we know them.
8. No final truth, for He is the Truth.
9. No Light of the World, for He is the Light of the World.
10. No hope beyond the grave, for He alone has risen from death.
11. No way to find God, no bridge, for He is the only Mediator between God and man (See I Timothy 2:5).
12. No Holy Spirit of God to give the power of new life and transmit His message to a lost world.

If Jesus had not come, we would be in the dark about a lot of things. This world would long ago have sunk into the swamp of depravity, anarchy, and ruin. But He did come and turned on the light, offering abundant life to all who believe in Him.

# CHAPTER 7

# REAL SHEPHERD

**P**salm 23 is ageless. People everywhere have learned to love the word picture of this beautiful poem. It is the Great Shepherd and His care for the sheep that is pictured here. Life – everybody's life – is going to have its trials and dangers, and the valley of the shadow of death. Here is a Shepherd-guide who has traveled the way we go and knows all the roads. He has the resources we need. He has the ability to protect, to shelter, and to provide a table of bounty – even in the presence of the enemy. He knows each of His sheep by name. He knows our personal cares and problems. This Shepherd gave His very life for the welfare of His sheep. And, risen from the dead, He continues to give His life for them as "…He ever liveth to make intercession for them" (Hebrews 7:25).

The Lord Jesus said, "I am the Good Shepherd…" (John 10:11). Multitudes have tried Him and proven Him. "All we like sheep have gone astray; we have turned everyone to his own way…" (Isaiah 53:6). The end of a stray sheep is always ruin, but the sure Good Shepherd can rescue him and bring him back.

Of course, there are other shepherds vying for the sheep. People are enticed to follow all kinds of philosophies, teachings and religions. Many will follow the crowd, or their own peers who are also straying. Many stubbornly act as their own shepherd, led around by their own appetite. Like the dog that chases his tail but never goes anywhere. his only accomplishment is going around in circles.

"Vanity, vanity, all is vanity" (Ecclesiastes 12:8).

At the end of the road, great danger waits for any who follow the wrong shepherd. Why follow a philosophy of life that has ended in hopeless confusion for so many when we could be led by the One who cannot fail?

- He is the only sinless one, so is the perfect example.
- He is motivated by pure love for us, so is interested in our need.
- He knows all things, so we cannot get lost.
- He has unlimited riches, so can meet all our needs.
- He has unlimited power, so can protect from any harm.
- He paid the supreme price for our ransom, erasing all condemnation.
- He rose from the dead and is now exalted to the highest heaven.

So, why follow a loser? Safety and security are things we all need. Faith lays claim on the Good Shepherd and says, "The Lord is my shepherd..." (Psalm 23:1).

# CHAPTER 8

# THE REAL CLIMAX

Jesus Christ was an amazing fact of history, a completely unique man among men.

Jesus Christ is an amazing fact of the present. He lives today, and many around this world are proving Him real in daily life.

Jesus Christ is an amazing fact of the future. The day will come when He will command the focus of the world. Any consideration of Him must take into account this major subject of the Bible, often prophesied, and referred to in both Old and New Testaments.

Over 2500 years ago, Daniel wrote down an incredible outline of four great world empires that would dominate history from his day to our day, incredible because of the accuracy of the outline in fulfillment. He also described conditions at the end of the age.

Then 2000 years ago, the Lord Jesus, responding to questions from His followers, gave certain signs and indicators of the progress and end of the age, climaxing with His return. Now, after all these centuries, we can see how accurate He was as events and conditions take shape as He said. The writers of the New Testament, Paul, Peter, John, all wrote much about His second coming. In writing the final book of the Bible, The Revelation, John used a word that contemporary writers use often – "Apocalypse" – which is from the Greek meaning to uncover, to make manifest, to reveal. Men usually associate the word with a terrible, fearsome, worldwide catastrophe because when Jesus comes again and is "revealed," He will judge this world and clean it up, setting things right. Throughout the Bible, writers such as Ezekiel, Isaiah, Zechariah, and Malachi all speak of the second coming of Jesus. On average, it is the subject of one in every 20 verses in the New Testament.

So why are there many churches where we rarely, if ever, hear about it? Why are there so many preachers who cannot speak of so grand a subject? The early churches called it "the blessed hope" for which we are admonished to be looking (Titus 2:13).

Since the Bible is true and since Jesus is truth personified, we can expect that soon – any day or week now – the Son of God will return to earth according to His promise (John 14:3). Are you ready? Are you following the Great Shepherd? Do not risk being left behind.

Could we be living in the final days before history climaxes with His coming?

If the predictions written in the Bible, and especially the prophecies of Jesus describing the course of history and the end of the age had been hidden for a thousand years and discovered just recently, it would be astonishing news. Men would say, "What an amazingly accurate picture." Jesus spoke of earthquakes in various places. They have increased dramatically. Jesus predicted wars and rumors of wars. No comment is needed. He spoke of heat so intense it melts the very elements, and we know today how that could happen. Read Revelation 16:9 and II Peter 3:10-11. People will love only themselves and their appetites. The Bible predicted self-willed, disobedient children, widespread greed, the breakdown of sexual morality and family ties, wild proliferation of false religions and would-be Christs, and with it all "...knowledge shall be increased" (Daniel 12:4). "Oh, well," they say, "things have always been like that." Maybe. But never with the alarming acceleration we are witnessing.

As of this writing, one in five American women will be sexually abused by age 18. Abortion kills 1 1/2 million babies in America every year, 98 percent of them for reasons other than rape or to save the mother. There are financial and political scandals, bloodshed, and violence. Oh, hum! What is new?

"But as the days of Noah were, so shall also the coming of the

Son of Man be" (Matthew 24:37). Like the prodigal son, contemporary man puts as much distance between himself and God as he can. He spends all he can of money, character, morality, honor, and hope, until life is a shambles and he is in moral poverty. Comparatively few see the drift and rise up to go to the Father and home.

The Bible predicted that perilous times would come – perilous because men would be lovers of their own selves (II Timothy 3:1-2). Following that prophetic pronouncement, a list of 17 vices grow out of that kind of self-centeredness, which never produces positive results. The Old Testament prophet adds, "…his soul that is lifted up is not upright in him…" (Habakkuk 2:4).

If such warnings and predictions, by their familiarity, serve only to dull our senses, then we contribute to our own judgment. Followers of Jesus remember His promise that when things get their worst, His coming is near.

The second coming of Jesus is rightly called "the blessed hope." "Looking for that blessed hope, and the glorious appearing of the great God and our Savior, Jesus Christ" (Titus 2:13). Why is His coming called the blessed hope?

The Bible gives two basic reasons for His coming to earth. The first was accomplished at His first coming. The second will be accomplished when He comes again.

The first reason, "…thou shalt call His name Jesus; for He shall save His people from their sins" (Matthew 1:21). The meaning of the name, Jesus, is Savior. He was "…manifested to take away our sins…" (I John 3:5). He was manifested to "…destroy the works of the devil" (I John 3:8). He came "…to seek and to save that which was lost" (Luke 19:10). He came "…to minister, and to give His life a ransom for many" (Matthew 20:28).

The second reason will be accomplished when He comes again. "He shall be great…and the Lord God shall give unto Him the throne of his father, David. And He shall reign over the house of Jacob forever; and of His kingdom there shall be no end" (Luke 1:32-33).

For a thousand generations, men have dreamed of a perfect world. Long before Jesus came the first time, God had promised King David that one of his descendants would reign on a throne on this earth. The prediction was a major theme of the Old Testament prophets. For example, Daniel, 500 years before Christ, envisioned "one like the Son of Man came with the clouds of heaven, and came to the Ancient of Days, and they brought him near before him. And there was given Him dominion, and glory, and a kingdom, that all people, nations, and languages should serve Him..." (Daniel 7:13-14). His kingdom is described as a time of prosperity and peace, without crime or disease, with conditions like Eden. Obviously we are not there yet. Indeed the opposite would describe our world today as mankind in cynicism turns increasingly to himself and his appetites. Sometimes politicians use catch phrases like "a New World order." But each one fails, and will fail until our rightful King arrives to clean up our disasters and bring in His righteousness.

At His first coming they tried to make Him King. As they witnessed the marvels of His speech ("never man spoke like this man") and the incredible marvel of His miracles, they considered Him as one who could free them from bondage to Rome and meet all their physical and/or monetary needs. At His triumphal entry, they cried in unified chorus, "Blessed be the King who cometh in the name of the Lord..." (Luke 19:38). After the feeding of the 5,000 men, plus women and children there on the hillside, they intended to "...take Him by force, to make Him a King..." (John 6:15). But the time was not right. He would first be King of the heart before a king political. He must pay man's sin debt through His substitution for us on the cross. He must conquer our chief enemy, death, by His resurrection. Then, after His gospel is preached around the world and His family is complete, He will come again as King of Kings.

# CHAPTER 9

# REAL TRUTH

Catalogues, catalogues. The mailbox is flooded with catalogues and advertisements. One promotion tries to entice me to send for a book, telling how its author made a million dollars in just a few months, doing almost nothing. I think the truth is he made it selling books to the gullible.

Another wants me to send for a book titled, "How To Do Everything Better." Perhaps I should give one to each of the kids!? I have not seen that book, but the advertisement speaks of handling credit cards, real estate, banks, and the IRS. I suppose there would be advice for marital relationships, computers, and dog handling too. Surely it would offer good advice for dieting, exercising, and stomach trimming. Perhaps even growing hair on a bald head. Maybe I will send for that book after all!

The Bible is the book of all books: the catalogue of catalogues. It tells us how to acquire real life, how to live it, and how to keep it forever. If we really want to do things better, then we should begin today by taking a serious look at God's Word and making it a part of our daily schedules. A million people depend on it for accurate information about living – subjects like handling money, raising children, and building relationships. It covers all the things that really matter.

Most importantly, it tells us what we need to know about God and our relationship to Him. I meet people who say, "Oh, yes, I believe the Bible," yet they seldom read it. How do you know whether you believe it if you have not read it?

In case you are new to it, begin your look with the Gospel of John. Read that one book through two or three times. Then go to the little book of I John and read it two or three times. Be sure to do what it says. Then, the book of Proverbs tells you how to handle the affairs of life. And find a Bible-believing, practicing church, which can help you answer your questions. The book of answers tells you to **do** it right, and **how** to do it right. It describes to you a Friend who will walk with you and lead you. "And thine ears shall hear a word behind thee, saying, This is the way, walk ye in it, when you turn to the right hand, and when you turn to the left" (Isaiah 30:21).

I spoke with a man who claimed, "Yes, I do believe the Bible, but it has a lot of mistakes." Apparently he had not figured out the contradiction in his statement. Can you believe a book that is full of mistakes? There is clearly the touch of the supernatural in the Bible. Can God make mistakes? Here is the one book, religious or otherwise, that stands unique from, and far above all the others. No other writing, religious or otherwise, has so profoundly influenced the world, improved the lives of millions, or brought such comfort and direction to multitudes. Throughout its pages, it claims to be the Word of God, Himself. If that claim is true, how then can it have a lot of mistakes? The critics do not answer the simple challenge, "Show me."

Does God make mistakes? Does He keep His Word? Is He true? Does He change? "I am the Lord; I change not..." (Malachi 3:6). He does not need to change because He knows the end from the beginning. He is never surprised by the development of an unforeseen event. Furthermore, He cannot change for He is immutable. If He could or did change, it would of necessity be for the better, or for the worse. If He changed for the better, it would mean that He was not perfect to start with. If He changed for the worse, it would mean that He is not as good as He was before He changed!

My guess is that men's main problem with the Bible is that it condemns too many things we want to do. Our sin has made us rebels against the One who loves us the most, and who wants and can do the best for us.

Some preachers claim the Bible is outdated and doesn't contain moral standards in dealing with homosexuality, abortion, or promiscuity. What kind of preachers are these? They worship man before God. "...If they speak not according to this word, it is because there is no light in them" (Isaiah 8:20).

I asked a certain pastor, "Do you believe the Bible is inspired of God?" He answered, "I think it is inspired, but not inerrant." Now, that is a great example of doubletalk. Why would anybody walk across the street to hear a preacher whose God could not speak without error?

We know that Almighty God is final Truth and that He "cannot lie" (Titus 1:2). "All scripture is given by inspiration of God..." (II Timothy 3:16). The Greek word there means "God breathed". The Bible's claim throughout is that God breathed out and into human writers the words of scriptures. Moreover it promises that it will be preserved forever. Sometimes we hear it said that God originally inspired His word, but it has been corrupted through the centuries, so it may not be God's Word today. In answer, Jesus said, "Heaven and earth shall pass away, but my words shall not pass away" (Matthew 24:35). Peter adds, "the Word of God... liveth and abideth forever," and "endureth forever" (I Peter 1:25).

To suggest that the Bible may have errors is to destroy any solid foundation for faith. Faith becomes a wisp of fantasy and wishful thinking. We cannot simply visualize or wish something into reality. Without a dependable word from God, humanity has neither anchor nor rudder. Every one of us can formulate our own ideas, ideals, and standards, even though they may directly contradict each other, and declare them as truth, "as long as it works for you." All standards of moral right and wrong fall because there is no standard. Ultimately, any real knowledge of right and wrong is lost.

If the clear claim to inspiration, and therefore to accuracy, is not true, then the Bible is not true or dependable. If it is not true in one place, why is it in another place? We must conclude that either God has not spoken to His creation or, if He has, He has not spoken correctly, or has not spoken clearly enough, or perhaps He has failed to preserve His Word for our times. Some even believe that God has gone to sleep, or has no interest at all in human affairs. We would not presume to think such evil of our Maker.

Jesus said, "...the word that I have spoken, the same shall judge him in the last day" (John 12:48). When we at last stand before the Bible's author, will it not be best to have believed and lived His Word?

I have heard another complaint something like this, "There are so many different interpretations of the Bible, and everybody has a different idea about it." It becomes almost an accusation against the Book (and so against its author) that it was not written clearly enough for us to understand and agree about it. I have, more than once, quoted a clear sentence of the Bible to someone who responded, "Well, that depends on how you interpret it." Some have despaired of finding the truth almost before they start looking.

The fact is that this great confusion of conflicting beliefs about Christ and the Bible is not the fault of the Book, but of its readers. If a person with some bias does not want to believe what the Bible says, yet desires to hold some sort of reverence for it, he can just decide that it means something other than what it clearly says.

Consider these basic truths from the scriptures and judge their clarity:

1. "All have sinned, and come short of the glory of God" (Romans 3:23).
2. "...There is none that doeth good, no, not one" (Psalm 14:3).
3. God "...loved us and sent His Son" (I John 4:10).
4. Jesus said, "...I am the way, the truth, and the life; no man cometh unto the Father, but by me" (John 14:6).
5. "There is one God, and one mediator between God and men, the man, Christ Jesus" (I Timothy 2:5).
6. "Now is Christ risen from the dead..." (I Corinthians 15:20).
7. "...This same Jesus, who is taken up from you into heaven, shall so come in like manner as you have seen Him go into heaven" (Acts 1:11).
8. "Believe on the Lord Jesus Christ, and thou shalt be saved..." (Acts 16:31).

Such statements are just as clearly written numerous times throughout the Bible. They are not ambiguous. Each is subject to just one honest interpretation. A thousand translations or religious cults cannot change their easily-understood meanings. Abraham Lincoln was credited with saying, "It is not what I don't understand about the Bible that troubles me, but what I do understand." The way to find God is to take His Word at face value and obey what He says.

It is so easy to be careless about spiritual matters. Should I say it is natural? Our focus is on materials and pleasures that we can see, touch, and enjoy today. Indeed, attitudes toward the Bible often go beyond carelessness. It can be a nuisance that irritates. The slightest suggestion of God and His Word is enough to cause some to feel harassed and badgered. They want no finger pointing to the sinful lifestyle they enjoy.

Yet, the Great God who made us loves us and continues to invite us to Himself through His Word. This Book explains all we know about life and death. It is the final and best authority on how to be happy, living life to the fullest, both here and hereafter.

Here are "three R's" that describe three different ways to approach God: Ritualism, Relativism, and Realism. Ritualism focuses on and demands prescribed religious form, ceremony, and ritual. The ritualist does not feel right if ritual is missing. Yes, the Almighty Creator is majestic and holy and must be worshipped with deep and serious earnestness. He is most certainly worthy of our best. We would not attend a White House banquet carelessly, or in our work clothes. On such special occasions, we should try to practice proper ethics and protocol.

But in approaching God, too often the form and ritual is expected to work some magic, doing the work of pleasing God. Only a broken and contrite heart can do that. The Son of God completed all the "work" of redemption. So we come to Him, "Not by works of righteousness..." (Titus 3:5), but by sincere faith in Christ.

Relativism considers morality and truth to be variables. Here, there are no absolutes. The theory is expressed and practiced constantly. Statements such as, "When in Rome, do as the Romans;" "It may be wrong for you, but it is okay for me;" "The situation decides whether the act is right or wrong;" "If it does not hurt anyone else, there is nothing wrong with it." Relativism dreams of a god who is not holy and who could care less if his creatures are. Relativism takes God off His throne and tries to sit there itself to please its own appetites and tastes.

Realism deals with facts that can be demonstrated. One demonstrated fact is the fallen nature we all know. Children do not have to be taught how to lie, or throw a temper tantrum. Yes, there are a lot of "good" people around, and the good ones readily admit to imperfection. Another demonstrated fact is that *God is*. "The fool hath said in his heart, There is no God" (Psalm 14:1). Blue skies, green grass, immeasurable heavens, laws of nature, all demonstrate Him with a thousand voices. And, God has spoken (and is speaking) in His miracle book. The Bible stands completely unique in all literature. It has totally revolutionized millions of lives. And, finally, Jesus Christ the Lord died to pay the sinner's debt and then rose in triumph from death. These are facts that are or have been demonstrated. One may ignore them, hate them, laugh at them, but reality continues. Jesus said, "Come unto me, all ye that labor and are heavy laden, and I will give you rest" (Matthew 11:28). Realism is better than ritualism or relativism. So, get real!

# CHAPTER 10

# REAL SIN

Is the human race basically good? Or is it basically bad? There are those who would not consider the latter as even a remote possibility. Sure, there are greedy people and liars, bloodshed, and wars, but still, they argue, mankind is basically good. It is the environment, poverty, poor education, poor parentage, or too harsh discipline that are our real problems, not our sinful natures, for goodness sake. So we are constantly told to believe in ourselves, to project ourselves, to think how good we are. So we make jokes of sin, laugh at it, and ridicule the very idea. But it does not go away. Sin continues to be the major embarrassment of human beings.

Some think that mankind is basically bad. Incorrigibly bad. The only time he is good is when he redefines morality to mean whatever he wants to be good is good. But in reality he is really bad, and, given time, will self-destruct. Jesus said, "If ye then, being evil, know how to give good gifts…" (Luke 11:13).

Perhaps mankind is both good and bad. Perhaps the Bible's assessment is acutely accurate, so that in his original condition, man was perfectly good. He certainly was not an animal, but possessed capabilities and an intellect far superior to anything else on earth. There were no negatives in him – hatred, greed, uncontrolled appetite, and self-centeredness – nothing like that. But then he disobeyed his maker, fell into sin, opened a Pandora's box, and introduced the cancer of sin into his posterity. What we are now, today, is a riddle. Traces and reflections of the original state are apparent. Man's superior intellect, his uniqueness, his spiritual potential are still there, but the shame of sin is there too, making him capable of horrible crimes against his fellow man. The best education, riches, or easy living does not solve the problem or cure the cancer of sin.

Basically good, yes, but also basically bad. The question is how to cure the bad? How to be rid of sin? How to pay the sin debt? How to forever defeat Satan, the ultimate cause of sin?

Satan. Is he only a scarecrow, a figment of fear, an invented story or a superstition? Or is there, in fact, an ultra evil personality intent on destroying good, ensnaring souls, and defeating truth? If there is not, will someone please explain the confusion of evil that swamps us – alcoholism, drug addiction, violence, international crisis on one front after another, the fanatical drive to destroy the moral standards of our world, family ruptures, disease, et cetera? Universal sin is demonstrable.

Don't look for answers to the question of Satan in the philosophies of humanism, or in the writings of the amoral. One thing is certain: The old deceiver, the devil, never tells the truth about himself.

Several words, each with its own shade of meaning, appear in the Bible to describe sin and wrong:

"Iniquity" is perverseness, wickedness, and depravity.
"Transgression" is rebellion, a willful violation.
"Trespass" is a false step, a blunder, a deviation from obedience.
"Sin" is wrongdoing, a falling short.

My friends and I watched from a distant hill as some men stopped to look at a sign that read, "Private Property, Keep Off." But they wanted to go where the sign clearly prohibited them. So they tore the sign off the tree, threw it into the brush, and proceeded.

The Book of God is the major "No Trespassing" sign. There are others. Illicit sex brings disease and remorse. Anger destroys relationships. Alcohol robs health and finances and greatly harms children. Gambling empties pockets and reputations. Yet there is this mysterious fascination that draws us to disregard all the warnings.

The problem of evil is best explained by one source of accurate information – the Bible. The enemy of man's soul began his career on earth early when he planted the seed of doubt in Eve's ear with the words, "Yea, hath God said?" He then appealed to her pride with the promise, "You shall be as God, knowing…" Finally he appealed to her appetite with fruit that was "good." You know the rest of the story. She gave to Adam who knowingly became a participant. Disobedience was rebellion against God, so they ran to hide from God among the trees of the garden.

Now we can trace those steps in all the crime and violence, and perversion, and over-reaching in what is known as sin. Satan is real, alive, and active.

The good news is his defeat has been secured and is sure. The Son of God has "cast him out" (John 12:31). Jesus Christ was virgin born, thus without a sin nature. He lived a sinless life, and so was a suitable substitute for us. He died a sacrifice, to pay in full our judgment for sin. Eternal, absolute justice was satisfied there. He came out of death and the grave in physical resurrection, thus conquering our great enemy, sin, its result, death and its author, Satan.

Sin is for real, a fact to be reckoned with. Satan is for real as the wicked enemy of good and the superior attendant of evil. Christ is for real, alive, well, and is today active in saving all who will come to put their faith in Him.

Most, if not all of us, are willing to tolerate our own faults, sins, and failures. We say to ourselves, "This bad habit I indulge in may be a vice, but overall I am not bad. I may be blunt, but I mean well. Maybe I curse and swear, but that's my only bad habit."

Recently I observed a man talking with no one around him. When I asked him, "Who are you talking to?" he responded, "Myself, because no one else will listen!" So we talk to ourselves to convince ourselves that we are good. But the great Judge sees and hears all. He is not easily fooled!

Remember, the rules of God are a unit. "For whosoever shall keep the whole law, and yet offend in one point, he is guilty of all" (James

2:10). Perhaps I have never murdered anyone (6th Commandment), yet if I have coveted something (10th Commandment), I am guilty of breaking God's Law, all the same. Break one leg of the table and you've broken the table. Break one of the commandments of God and you are guilty of all. That is a heavy load.

A young couple, all happy and starry-eyed, entered the pastor's office. A wedding was in their plans. Any suggestion that one day the flower might fade and wither in a crumpled marriage was met with a vehement, "Oh, no! Not us!" Others maybe, but this relationship was cemented in eternal love. How very sad to see in a few swift years the rupture they thought impossible. Behind all the family wreckage so troubling to us lies a deep problem of sin and the decline in the stabilizing principles of Godliness. Separate from God is separate from righteousness.

Once, while in college, I worked as a welder's helper. I never became a welder, as that was not my goal, but I learned to recognize and admire the vital importance of a good, strong weld. Steel columns welded to support the dock must withstand the terrific force of moving ice and heavy seas, pipe welded to pipe to transport natural gas under pressure. If the weld is not good, lives are endangered. The inspector performs a test subjecting the welds to severe stress and bends to see whether they will hold.

There is a spiritual welding, essential to goodness in life and to life everlasting.

Those marriage vows, spoken with emotion and good intention, made "for better or worse" were thought to be permanent, but when a little of "worse" came, the weld was broken. The stress test often breaks our moral integrity. We all need an encounter of faith with the Great Welder, by whom we become inseparably joined to Him and the standards of morality laid down in His Word.

Our world is focused on rights, pleasures, and dollars – not necessarily in that order. We are told that happiness comes in those areas. It is something we owe ourselves – and the government owes us, also. Watching thousands of hours of artificial lifestyles and sex scenes on the screen, we come to think of those things as reality (which they are not) and the sum of happiness and fulfillment (which they are not). We glorify, "Do it my way." We elevate and promote self. Feed it. Pander it. We have "I trouble." To be success-oriented has certain nobility about it, but too often it has developed into pure greed, from the halls of politics, to financial institutions, to our homes.

Getting the people out of the ghetto won't solve our social problems; getting the ghettos out of the people will. In other words, we have heart trouble and need a change there. Jesus said, "For out of the heart proceed evil thoughts, murders, adulteries, fornications, thefts, false witness, blasphemies. These are the things which defile a man..." (Matthew 15:19-20). The heart is the seat of emotions and attitudes. It must be remolded so that we will be motivated to act and speak in moral decency, not degeneracy; in goodness and honesty, not greed; in love, not bitterness. Such a makeover is the offer made by the great heart specialist, Jesus Christ. He said to Nicodemus, a Jewish official, "...Ye must be born again" (John 3:7). The Bible term is regeneration, which means to make over. That is what the Lord Jesus does for the person who accepts Him as his Savior from sin, and faith in God becomes the control factor in life. At the new birth we receive the gift of a brand new life that is everlasting. "Therefore, if any man be in Christ, he is a new creation; old things are passed away; behold, all things are become new" (II Corinthians 5:17).

# CHAPTER 11

# REAL MORALITY

What is morality? What is immorality? I hear talk of "family values," but no one wants to define them other than ambiguously. What is right or wrong? In a self-centered, promiscuous society, these concepts cannot be defined. Moral rights and wrongs vary according to individuals, places, and times. Supposedly, the major consideration is the effect the act has on another person. The so-called "victimless crime" is nobody else's business (they say).

But there is the law of influence, meaning that there are really no "victimless crimes." "None of us liveth to himself…" (Romans 14:7). We say, "I can control my drinking." Maybe, but if we are part of the traffic, we contribute to the problem. We do not promote its cure. Adultery, homosexuality, pornography, et cetera, all have an undeniably negative effect on others. Exposure and practice of vice promotes experimentation with vice.

Moreover, and more important, evil is evil inherently, because our Maker says so. Of course, if we have no Creator, and if we are the products of evolutionary chance, then what the Bible says about morality can be trashed. But since God created us, then spoke to us in His Word, we do possess an unchanging standard for deciding questions of moral action which, by the way, has been the source of America's goodness.

Is gambling right, wrong, or neutral? Gambling is essentially wrong. It is based on greed and plays to man's baser nature. It seeks to get something for nothing, and is usually accompanied by other vices. Still, it is glamorized and becomes increasingly popular. We hear of "addictive gamblers" as though they cannot help themselves. The truth is, they gamble because they love it. Self-focus. When something rises to the level of addiction, we should raise the question of its morality.

I heard a man, seeking to justify his gambling, say with a shrug of indifference, "All of life is a gamble." That is not true, for life is not a gamble. It is a gift, and there are fixed laws that guarantee the outcome of actions.

For example, we reap what we sow. Plant potatoes; reap potatoes. Simple. Happens every time. It is axiomatic. No gamble there! And it is a moral law as well as a farmer's law. Sow corruption; reap corruption. Sow the wind; reap the whirlwind. Wild oats produce wild oats. Live an immoral life and reap the fruit of confusion, disillusionment, and disappointment. Want to know why some kids are insecure, wild, or uncontrollable? Check out the seed sown by the parents. Life is not a gamble. There is sure profit in righteous living. There is certain loss in unrighteous living. Live for Christ and we cannot lose. Without Him, we cannot win.

"For the wages of sin is death, but the gift of God is eternal life through Jesus Christ, our Lord" (Romans 6:23). No gamble. The rule is fixed, tested, and proven. Notice three contrasts in that statement:

1. Wages versus Gift – We earn the first. We simply receive the second.
2. Sin versus God – Sin is opposite of God. Sin is behind the wages. God is behind the gift. We make the choice.
3. Death versus Eternal Life – One is conscious existence apart from God. The other is conscious existence in the presence of God (heaven). Forever. The gift comes "through Jesus Christ our Lord" who came to reconcile us to God.

Is the sex act wrong, right, or neutral? There was a time, not so very long ago, when that three-letter word was not spoken in a mixed crowd and was an improper subject for the family newspaper.

But now, when parents rightly object to exposing their children to its promotion in the school library, the editor yells, "Censorship!" Say, how we've changed. And some think we have not changed enough. Indeed, it appears that some would have us all live in a nudist camp with free and open action in the sex department – like dogs, or cattle in the stockyard. At least Adam and Eve had enough sense to feel shame for their nakedness.

This crowd writes scornfully of the Puritans. The Victorians were too prudish! Hah! They did not have AIDS and other sexually transmitted diseases. Today we have come to the opposite extreme with a dog-style morality, trying to erase moral decency, distorting the proper place of sex, and teaching perverted ideas to kids in school. We reap the fruit of massive social problems, enormous expense, and broken lives that threaten our social structure.

Our Maker knew what He was talking about when He said, "Thou shalt not commit adultery." Consenting adults or not, sexual impurity is sin – and be sure your sin will find you out (Numbers 32:23)! True morality means, and has always meant:

- Sexual relations are exclusively for married men and women.
- Homosexual activity is forbidden.
- Marriage is for life.
- The monogamous, loving family unit is the Creator's design and the foundation of a decent society.

Morality is demonstrated in words. "…For out of the abundance of the heart the mouth speaketh" (Matthew 12:34). Watch your language! The 3rd Commandment warns, "Thou shalt not take the name of the Lord thy God in vain." Strange it is that it has become so common for people to do that very thing, using the God-given gift of speech to dishonor God. And why is the name of Jesus so often used in profanity? The name of any other famous person is not used like that.

Our speech has become so very crude and vulgar. Television producers seem to consider vulgarity a virtue. Women, not to say ladies, will use language that burns the ears. Men with college degrees seem incapable of expressing themselves without cursing. Teenagers use rotten words – possibly with the warped idea that adding such "spicy" words to their vocabulary makes them somebody. Language has become a cesspool of filthy, dirty, vulgar, and shameful words. Air pollution! In a spurt of anger, we hear, "To hell with it!" or "Go to hell!" Jesus said that hell is a place of torment where one never loses consciousness, separated forever from God and good. Do we want anyone to go there?

I can tell what shape your soul is in by your speech. Nothing illustrates the moral poverty of society, and our lack of sensitivity more clearly than the increasing use of vulgarity and profanity in speech. Ask yourself:

- Is it a mark of manliness or womanliness, or intelligence?
- Is it a mark of self-control?
- Do you think it impresses others favorably?
- Does it make you happy to so dishonor God?
- Does it contribute to the moral good of our country?
- Do you use it in the presence of a pastor?

"Let the words of my mouth, and the meditation of my heart, be acceptable in thy sight, O Lord, my strength, and my redeemer" (Psalm 19:14).

Discussions about morals and morality make us think of the thing we call conscience. Every man, woman, and accountable child has one. Our conscience is as real a part of us as our beating hearts. Rich and poor, corrupt and honest, Chinese and African, educated and uneducated, Democrat and Republican, everybody has a conscience.

Our conscience is God's watchdog that bothers us when we consider an evil action. As one little boy said, "It is what makes you tell your mother before your sister does." It is God's policeman that accuses of wrong. It stands on your shoulder, close by your ear whether you are driving, eating, partying, telling a story, or filing your tax statement. You cannot escape it. Sometimes it has driven to suicide.

But be careful, the conscience is easily damaged. We can ignore it – and do wrong in spite of it. Do that repeatedly and we soon blunt its edge so that it does not perform as designed. If we persist in acting contrary to our conscience, we will gradually lose that critical sense of right and wrong. We witness that happening in our permissive generation. Exaggerations and lies become habits. High school and college students cheat on exams without a qualm. The adulterer indulges his lust until he is persuaded it is the norm. A high schooler bragged about "sleeping around." When asked if her conscience was troubled, she replied, "Nah, it used to bother me, but not any more!" Actions and speech that were perversions not so long ago are now accepted, and dissenters are branded with discrimination or censorship. Our nation is having its conscience seared and nothing short of a spiritual renewal can save it.

It is the function of an enlightened conscience to tell us when we have sinned. It also tells us that sin must be atoned for. We find that belief in the most primitive areas on earth. The prophet Micah echoed the universal cry when he said, "...Shall I give my first-born for my transgression, the fruit of my body for the sin of my soul?" (Micah 6:7).

God's answer is the cleansing blood of the crucified and risen Savior to clean the conscience and give peace to the soul (Hebrews 9:14). It has often been said that America is in desperate need of a spiritual renewal. For too long we have been molded by secularism, which has been proven incompetent to meet our needs. It is not a booming economy and wealth that solves moral sickness. We need a spiritual awakening. Finding God involves submitting the conscience to His standards. Agree with Him regarding sin and goodness and morality. May David's prayer be ours, "Teach me thy way, O Lord; I will walk in thy truth; unite my heart to fear thy name" (Psalm 86:11). The Lord Jesus promised the winning style, "Seek ye first the kingdom of God, and His righteousness, and all these things shall be added unto you" (Matthew 6:33).

How often we hear that "Times have changed." The speaker is either deploring the moral slippage, or, happy about it, he is trying to shame those holding to traditional moral values. Because we live in a changing world, they say, we need to loosen our moorings.

There used to be certain words, acts, and activities that everybody considered non-moral and because they were immoral, it was considered that their practice would contribute to the decline of society and the forfeiture of God's favor – which was important in those days. Churches consistently spoke out against such activities, and tried to raise the flag of righteousness. God was God. Even profane people held a measure of reverence for Him. His Word, the Bible, was highly esteemed, providing a standard of decency and morality. Sex was monogamous. It was part of the married life only. It was heterosexual. Men whose lives were a moral shambles off the athletic or political field did not attain hero status. Wheaties was the breakfast of champions, and booze was not advertised as the winner's choice.

Then we fell in love with Hollywood and television. We watched its artificial lifestyle and promotion of sin by the hour. Vicariously, we allowed a liberal media to mold us. By its own admission, Hollywood pushes the moral envelope, appealing to man's basest nature, stimulating emotions, luring viewers, and selling programs. Churches became religious chameleons, motivated by growth, philosophy, and pragmatism. The major prohibition is that they offend no one (even the devil). Preachers became like kitchen blenders, putting in a bit of everything and delivering hash. We accepted the anti-God message and pushed Him out of school!

So now we are enlightened. Times have changed. Purity and fidelity are now a subject for crude jokes that, not long ago, would have been censored out of a radio broadcast. We are so enlightened that we do not know what we believe! And we are proud of that! Many are proudly calling themselves "agnostic" which means "ignorant." Here are educated people who would be properly indignant if we called them ignorant, who are proud of their ignorance of their Creator. The Apostle Peter long ago spoke of those who are "willfully ignorant."

Our unbelieving world is adrift with no rudder. We scratch our heads in confusion with moral-related problems. What do we do with the constantly increasing incidence of rape, child abuse, pornography, AIDS, suicide, substance abuse, abortion, dishonesty, corruption, overflowing jails, and asylums, ad infinitum?

Statistics are alarming. Published numbers of the increase in property crimes, juvenile arrests, murders, and rapes should be enough to awaken us from our spiritual stupor.

Suggested cures are interesting: sports activities, study groups, curfews, some way to "get kids off the streets." We have seen and participated in these efforts. No one should be cynical about the value of such social remedies; however, we should know by now that they are little more than band aids. Our problem is deeper and the disease more serious than a Tylenol fix.

Probably the most often suggested cure to our moral problems is education. When discussing serious social problems such as substance abuse or teenage pregnancy, we consider education as the solution about nine times out of ten. We are the best-educated people in the world. Education has become an idol. We think that if people are given the right information, they will make the right decisions. We think the answer to social ills is the accumulation of knowledge – more education, more explicit sex education given at the youngest age, re-education of convicts, sensitivity training, and so on.

The pursuit of knowledge is praiseworthy. Education is good for us. But there are a thousand illustrations to prove that, by itself, it can never solve social and moral problems. History has not produced a generation that was better educated than ours – and not one has had more serious social problems. It is glaringly obvious that a college degree does not make people want to do right, nor give them the ability to do right. They just do wrong with a bit more sophistication. Education by itself can lead to the pride of life and refusing to acknowledge our own limits or the real source of unchanging, authoritative truth.

It takes only a casual look at history, ancient to recent, to demonstrate that man's basic nature has a deep-seated malady. Continuous wars, murder, greed, stealing, deceit, and immorality is proof. "The heart is deceitful above all things, and desperately wicked..." (Jeremiah 17:9). As much as we moderns would like to think otherwise, humans have a bent to sin and are in need of a change of heart more than an education of the mind. The problem is not so much in the head as in the heart.

Our Creator God is a great heart doctor. "A new heart also will I give you, and a new spirit will I put within you…" (Ezekiel 36:26). Real truth must include God. Solomon said, "The fear of the Lord is the beginning of knowledge, but fools despise wisdom and instruction" (Proverbs 1:7). Subtract God from the picture, as we have tried to do, and we produce educated spiritual failures. How many years of failure will it take for us to learn that educating 10- or 12-year-olds in the art of sex and condoms is a no win? Or that educating teens about alcohol will not keep them from drinking? But let a person come to know the Great Shepherd, and he will soon experience the promise, "And I will put my spirit within you, and cause you to walk in my statutes, and ye shall keep my judgments, and do them" (Ezekiel 36:27).

Morality is an issue of the heart and not some characteristic that is molded from the outside. Mandates or laws cannot govern it. We must have laws to regulate recognized evils, such as thievery and murder. Yet the thief will be a thief, law or no law. There is a rather widespread belief that "Christians" need to gain control of the government in some way. It is neither by force of arms, nor by controlling the political system, or in any way forcing our ideals on government, that we improve the present moral dilemma. That is not what we are commissioned to do. That is not what the early Christians did in the days of Rome. Yes, we should vote. Yes, we should be involved, raise the standard, and stand against moral evil. But if we pursue the "take over" policy, we are in immediate competition and conflict with all who may be on the other side. If it were possible to pass morality laws prohibiting substance abuse, cheating, lying, filthy language, and so on, we might have a society clean on the outside, by force, but unchanged foundationally – in the heart. Our commission is to witness to the power of the Gospel of Christ. There is conquering power in a life transformed by that power. The real way of success in the struggle against moral evil is for true Christians to live, act, and speak righteously. "That ye may be blameless and harmless, the sons of God, without rebuke, in the midst of a crooked and perverse nation, among whom you shine as lights in the world, holding forth the word of life…" (Philippians 2:15-16).

So, can we have morality without "religion"? It all depends on our concept of morality. If it is variable like the weather, changeable according to each person's likes and dislikes, fluctuating with the circumstances, then the only god we need for that kind of morality is ourselves. The logical end of that kind of morality is anarchy. But if morality is based on objective standards of right, as observed by nations throughout history – concepts like honesty, sexual purity, respect for the persons and properties of others, and the sanctity of human life – then it is true that a people without God will soon become a people without morality and in the end, a people without direction and without hope.

We are now witnesses to the fruit of a growing segment of society without God. Too many are despondent and desperate. Mind-altering drugs, alcohol, and the latest stuff on the street have mega-multiplied. Pharmacies offer shelves full of legal drugs to soothe us. Illicit sex, fatherless children, and suicide describe a society in trouble.

A policeman found a man on a bridge about to jump over the rail and kill himself. "Come now," said the officer, "things aren't that bad. Let's walk and talk it over." Thirty minutes later, they returned and both jumped over.

The moral picture of society is a disgrace. Concerned people in high places and little places are repeating, "Our country is in desperate need of a spiritual awakening." Crude vulgarity is acceptable speech. Pornography is readily available, from computer or television, and part of the diet of children in many homes. Sex outside marriage is more common than in marriage. One hundred thousand plus deaths from booze annually in America, and no one knows all the other damage and loss from alcohol. I think it was Shakespeare who said, "Alcohol is a poison men take into the mouth to steal away the brain." It is the only "disease" we allow to be sold in a bottle for profit.

For many, satisfying the various appetites of the body is the main reason for living. As we continue to devour our lusts, we will certainly consume ourselves.

No, there cannot be a moral, spiritual awakening without a return to God. There never has been. There never will be. To ignore God is ungodly. To make ourselves gods is fatal – in time and in eternity.

We've cultivated a relatively new philosophy called "no fault." I guess it means that there can be an accident – or a divorce – where no one is at fault. It is a rather mushy principle that runs through our various relationships. Seldom are we at fault or blameworthy about anything. If we are, we get paralysis of the tongue. The cartoon character said, "I used to be conceited, but I don't have any faults at all now."

Some disciplines do not conform to this "no fault" idea. In math, if the answer is wrong, it is wrong. A mistake in figuring results in an error. The science of geography is so precise the surveyor can establish an exact boundary. If he insists the corner is somewhere other than the legal description, there is an error. Somebody is at fault.

Yet, when it comes to morality or how to approach God and please Him, nobody could possibly be in error. Ten people in your neighborhood can go about that business in ten different ways and come in with ten different and opposing answers and nobody is wrong. They say we are all going to the same place; we just go by different roads! I am asked to respect some opinion, even though it is clearly contrary to truth. Imagine telling three people, each with a column of 20 figures, to add up the figures. One of the contestants decides to multiply; the other to divide. There will, of course, be three different results. All three cannot arrive at the same place.

There is a sin problem. There is a moral problem. As long as we refuse to deal with it in the way directed by our Creator God, there will be no checking the moral slide. We can laugh and scoff at the very suggestion that sin exists, but no amount of covering or denial will heal it. We must build a foundation of righteous principles in the soul that will work as an antidote for sin.

The parent who never seeks God and His righteousness should not be surprised if his child does not. The dad who curses God, using His name in vain, should expect his kids to do likewise. Alcoholics and gamblers can plan on their children following their examples. When integrity can be bargained, we needn't look for honesty in our offspring. If money is the goal in life, it will likely become the family's vain pursuit.

The prospector left this note in his pocket, "I lost my gun; I lost my horse; I am out of food. The Indians are after me, but I've got all the gold I can carry." "For what is a man profited, if he shall gain the whole world, and lose his own soul? Or what shall a man give in exchange for his soul?" (Matthew 16:26).

There has never been but one cure for our sin problem. The only rescue for a person, a family, a city, or a nation on the moral skids is, and always has been, a spiritual revival. The medication involves surrender – surrender to God who loves us and to His will that is always good. "And this is His commandment, that we should believe on the name of His Son, Jesus Christ..." (I John 3:23).

# CHAPTER 12

# REAL VALUE

It is hard to imagine someone selling his soul to the devil. Yet, there are those who make such a bizarre and extremely foolish deal. Remember Judas Iscariot? Far more common, but just as foolish, is to lose our soul by default, or by trading it off for the vain baubles the world has to offer. We could gain the whole world and lose our own soul, a bargain to regret forever.

Try to imagine or calculate the wealth of the whole world. What an enormous heap! Pile up all the banks, stock markets, factories, industries, automobiles, and satellites. Add on all the ships, aircraft, hotels, and Las Vegas. Pile on all the gold, diamonds, platinum, and uranium. Bring on the petroleum business and the oil and gas still in the ground, and don't forget the government's reserves. It is all bigger than imagination. Jesus Christ said that all of it together could not equal the value of our soul. All of this world's wealth will rust, burn, and fade away to emptiness. But our conscious soul is eternal. To live on, without end. And the redeeming blood of the Son of God has the purchasing power of all our souls. That is why the Bible calls it "precious" (I Peter 2:4-7).

To watch and listen to political debating and campaigning is interesting, to say the least. Among the various interests, promises, claims, and ideas, several important philosophies struggle for prominence. Economics, socio-political persuasions (socialism, conservatism, et cetera), and Biblical morality all compete for our ears. Which is most important for our national or local good? For many, it is clear: Biblical morality is way down on the list of priorities. Some insist that the candidate for public office should not be questioned about his family life, or that his record of moral virtue has nothing to do with his ability to govern.

Many of us would vehemently disagree. If he is not faithful to his spouse, can we expect him to be faithful in governing matters? Integrity is tested first at home. Economics is important. So are morality and God. The majority of us have some belief in God. Who is He? Is He awake? Attentive? If He is totally good, does He not hate evil? Is He not a God of holiness and justice? And does He not act in agreement with those qualities when He deals with nations – or with individuals?

Here is what He says: "Righteousness exalteth a nation, but sin is a reproach to any people" (Proverbs 14:34).

Travelers in foreign lands face the problem of currency exchange. Purchasing power fluctuates so wise travelers know to take a sufficient supply. There is a spiritual comparison. Christians are traveling in a foreign country. "Our citizenship is in heaven..." (Philippians 3:20). If we are going to meet the demands, the tests, the temptations of this country (i.e. this world), we need the supply of wealth from our home (i.e. heaven). Without it, we will not be successful here, or go home to heaven at the end of our tour.

Jesus spoke of "true riches". He meant riches toward God. He called the man a fool who "...layeth up treasures for himself, and is not rich toward God" (Luke 12:21).

This world's value system figures that the individual with his pile of money and toys is the most successful. "He who has the most toys wins." But without "true riches" it is all an empty husk. Vanity. Burnable. We cannot have true success in either country (earth or heaven) without the riches of God. Earth's wealth is worthless in heaven. "You can't take it with you." On the other hand, heavenly riches have great value in our pilgrimage through this world. We cannot convert earth's wealth to heaven's needs. We can use heaven's wealth for earth's needs. That is what the Apostle Paul meant when he said, "My God shall supply all your need according to His riches in glory by Christ Jesus" (Philippians 4:19).

On that exchange rate, there is an inflexible law wherein worldly values always decrease (entropy), while spiritual values always increase.

> "Every day my way grows brighter,
> The longer I serve Him, the sweeter He grows."
> – William J. Gaither

Now, it is possible to invest earthly wealth for heavenly returns. We can't take it with us, but we can send it on ahead! When we spend ourselves – or our dollars – to propagate the Gospel and win people for Christ, He does not forget that. "Henceforth there is laid up for me a crown of righteousness, which the Lord, the righteous judge, shall give me at that day; and not to me only, but unto all them also that love His appearing" (II Timothy 4:8).

Best of all, heaven's wealth is not something for which we must work to earn. It is free by faith. "The **gift** of God is eternal life through Jesus Christ, our Lord" (Romans 6:23). "Set your affection on things above, not on things on the earth" (Colossians 3:2).

Covetousness sounds bad! Money hungry. It sounds bad because it is bad. The word conjures up a greedy, avaricious weasel that is never satisfied. Few people would wish to describe themselves that way. They would not include covetousness as a desirable characteristic on a job application. But in our materialistic society, it surely is a common and troublesome trait.

Throughout the Bible, there are repeated warnings about this sin. The Ten Commandments forbid it (Exodus 20:17). It is defined as idolatry, and something that will keep you out of heaven (Ephesians 5:5). The Apostle Paul wrote, "For the love of money is the root of all evil..." (I Timothy 6:10), and predicted that the last days would be marked by an increase of covetousness (II Timothy 3:1-2).

Clearly, avarice has reached epidemic proportions. While nobody admits to being infected, it is obvious everywhere. It drives multitudes to strap themselves with credit payments for goodies they want but do not need. Popular religious evangelists preach a prosperity gospel (without Biblical foundation), while they collect money from the gullible who support their affluent lifestyles. Gambling, social security fraud, welfare fraud, food stamp fraud, scandals in financial institutions – all evidence the disease of covetousness. Sooner or later we learn its vanity. After years of raking or scraping for our little treasure, we discover what the Bible said long ago – it never satisfies. "…Beware of covetousness; for a man's life consisteth not in the abundance of the things which he possesseth" (Luke 12:15).

A preoccupation with material gain invariably leads to spiritual bankruptcy. If we need and desire a cure for covetousness, read the advice of Jesus in Matthew 6:24-33, which begins with, "You cannot serve God and money", and ends like this, "Seek ye first the kingdom of God, and His righteousness, and all these things shall be added unto you."

Money! A weird, wild, uncanny, mystical necessity in living. Sometimes it is beautiful like an angel. Often it is as ugly as sin. An uncontrolled wild animal will likely be troublesome. Harnessed and controlled, it will be useful. We must give attention to our goods – "Be thou diligent to know the state of thy flocks, and look well to thy herds" (Proverbs 27:23). But beware, lest money becomes so big that we see nothing else. We must have some to survive in this world, but it can easily master us. It demands attention, and the more we have, the more demanding. It causes worry, controls actions, and affects relationships. It changes personalities. And the security it promises is false – like a man who leans against the wall to rest and a poisonous spider bites him. Here is a man who works and rakes for years to secure himself with insurance policies, stocks, and retirement benefits. He anticipates years of pleasure from his investments. Then he has a stroke, a heart attack, cancer; "…whose shall those things be, which thou hast provided?" (Luke12:20).

One way or another, as sure as the sunrise, money will fail our trust. It is a poor place for faith. King Tutankhamen had it buried with him. The gold was there for the grave robbers but it did not help King Tut. "Riches are not forever" (Proverbs 27:24). Nobody has ever found God there.

For those who have already traded true, eternal riches for the false security of temporary riches, such warnings do not mean much. But for anyone who sees the emptiness of temporary riches, the abundant life is available in Christ for the receiving. "He that trusteth in his riches shall fall, but the righteous shall flourish like a branch" (Proverbs 11:28).

The most important thing in this world has to be how to get out of this world alive. Our allotted time here is so short. The life beyond is forever. The Bible is the greatest book ever to be offered, and its priority message is eternal life and how to find it. Many different subjects are covered in this greatest of books. It is the authority on such things as personal morality, human relationships, dealings with government, finances, and, of course, the supernatural. But the subject pressed above all others is personal salvation. Jesus said, "Ye must be born again." Paul wrote, "We pray you in Christ's stead, be ye reconciled to God." Peter spoke, "There is none other name under heaven, given among men, whereby ye must be saved." John pressed it, "He that believeth not the Son shall not see life, but the wrath of God abides on him."

If salvation is not the most important thing, these were all mistaken. The incarnation of Christ had no meaning, and His going to the cross as our substitute was useless. "But now is Christ risen from the dead..." (I Corinthians 15:20), and the validity of the Bible message is established.

Many consider Christ and His salvation as a sort of supplemental accessory to life. Like pin striping on a car; some like it and some do not. It is not considered essential to one's proper function. To others, He is like a spare tire. We would not drive far without one, but we rarely think of it, or its condition, until we have a flat.

But if there is, in fact, an after-death existence, if there is a righteous God out there, if life in its best quality and eternal quantity can be ours in Christ as the Bible teaches, then salvation must be the single most important subject in all our experience.
Do not leave this world without it!

# CHAPTER 13

# REAL FAITH

B elieving God is essential to finding God. If we do not believe Him, we dishonor Him. I do not say to believe *about* Him, that is, to believe in His existence – many who are lost believe that – but to believe God in the sense that we believe what God says, depend on and trust in His words.

True faith is always in the company of repentance. These are two sides of the coin. While distinct from each other, the one implies the other. They are not the same, but where one is, we will find the other. And the Bible demands both for salvation and conversion. "(God) now commands all men everywhere to repent," (Acts 17:30). "Believe on the Lord Jesus Christ, and thou shalt be saved…" (Acts 16:31). Paul's message declared, "repentance toward God, and faith toward our Lord Jesus Christ." (Acts 20:21).

The word, repent, means to change one's mind. In repenting, there is a rational decision to agree with God; that sin is evil and worthy of condemnation. Repentance involves a decision to turn away from sin. It is different from a psychological evaluation, or a stepped program of change.

The word, faith, means a conviction or persuasion that God is true and, therefore, worthy of complete trust. As a consequence, I make a rational decision to commit my life to the One in whom I have put my faith (i.e. the Lord Jesus Christ).

In repentance, I turn away from sin and self. In faith, I turn to the Savior. Both actions have to do with the will. They may or may not be accompanied by intense emotion, but we should not mistake "feelings" for either repentance or faith. We can "feel" great guilt for our sin, and yet not repent, or turn from it. Likewise, we may feel emotional about Christ while stopping short of being willing to completely trust Him. The question is not how do we "feel" but what will we do? Will we agree with God about that sin and turn from it, and turn to Christ? Jesus said that unless we repent, we will perish (Luke 13:3). He also promised that if we believe on Him, we will not perish, but have everlasting life (John 3:16).

This is a formula that has been around for a long time in God's dealings with us. About 4,000 years ago, old Abraham "believed God, and it was counted unto him for righteousness" (Romans 4:3). New Testament saints are saved by faith. "Being justified by faith, we have peace with God..." (Romans 5:1). Faith is the "victory that overcometh the world" (I John 5:4). It is faith that enables us to understand spiritual things (Hebrews 11:3). Faith is the hand that reaches out to receive that which God offers. The Lord commended a soldier for his great faith (Matthew 8:10). He reproved those whose faith was too small (Matthew 8:26). He rewarded some in accordance with the degree of their faith (Matthew 9:29). He attributed success to a person's faith (Luke 8:48).

He placed such a great emphasis on the importance of faith that His disciples, seeing it, learned well, and sought greater faith (Luke 17:5). We would be wise to do the same, remembering the directions given for growing our faith: "Faith cometh by hearing...the Word of God" (Romans 10:17). That means that if we consistently make God's Word a part of daily life and our director, faith will grow and be strong.

In Luke 18, Jesus told of a helpless widow who went to a judge for a just judgment against her oppressive adversary. He ignored her, but she, believing he could help her, persisted until he took her case and she was rewarded. Sometimes it may seem as though God does not respond to the prayers of those who believe Him, but He will! He looks for reality and earnestness. He is moved by our importunate prayer – and if He delays, we can be sure that in His love and wisdom, He has good reasons.

After He told that story, Jesus asked a provocative question. "When the Son of man cometh, shall He find faith on the earth?" (Luke 18:8). Let us make sure He does!

Two friends were discussing the questions and problems of life. One said wistfully, "I wish that I could have the strong faith that you have."

The beauty and value of faith are recognized everywhere. It is an essential dynamic in life, having great power. But it must be centered on the right object. People speak of faith as though it were a force in itself! Faith in faith. Believe something hard enough and it will be so. Common as that idea may be, it is fairyland talk – unreal and producing nothing. Faith must be grounded in truth, or else it is useless. Rightly focused, faith provides answers to the puzzles of life, puts muscle in moral resolves, builds iron in the will, and creates hope and joy in the heart. Faith knows how to pray and receives answers. Faith gives solid confidence for the future. Faith is an inner value system to keep us from crooked moral actions that threaten us.

But how do we get faith? Are some born with it while others are not? Is it a natural gift? Does one look for visions, or follow someone who said they had one? Cultivate some emotion? Investigate the occult? Meditate on the "inner self"?

True faith is born in the soul when we listen to God speaking in His Word. "These are written that you might believe..." (John 20:31). "Faith comes by hearing ...the Word of God" (Romans 10:17). The first step through the gate to a life of faith is to place our trust in the One who is the major subject of the Word, the Lord Jesus.

You might be a liberal or a conservative, Republican, Democrat, or Independent (I hope you are involved), but if your philosophy of life can be summed up in politics, secular education, economics, or business, you are on a dead-end street. Put faith in the winning object. It will mold your actions, your relationships, your outlook, your attitude, your dreams, and your face!

This statement provides a helpful principle: "See that ye refuse not Him that speaketh" (Hebrews 12:25a). The principle is that there is an intrinsic connection between a speaker and his words. To refuse the speaker is to refuse his speech. Conversely, to refuse the speech is to refuse the speaker. The man on the witness stand before the jury will not have a convincing testimony if he has a record of perjury. He may have perjured himself by his words. And when we call a person a liar, we impugn their very character.

A lot of people want to stand under the umbrella of Christianity without listening to or obeying the Great God who speaks through His eternal word. The Bible is His Word, but many churches and many "preachers" are not following it. Jesus asked, "Why call ye me, Lord, Lord, and do not the things which I say?" (Luke 6:46). He meant that it is a contradiction to claim Christianity while ignoring His word. When we reject the speech, we reject the speaker.

So then, the getting and building of faith involves the submission and surrender of self to the God who speaks. If I believe God, I must believe what God says. If I desire to hear God speak, I will read His word.

They say we cannot prove scientifically that God exists. Ah! Neither can we prove that He does not exist! Surely, there should be far more evidence that He does exist than evidence to the contrary – and such is the case. All it takes is an honest look: From the baby's cradle to the starlit sky, from the little bug to the great tree he crawls on, from the photo genius of the eye to the complex ocean with its purification process, the hydrology circuit from ocean to cloud to river to ocean, and a thousand more inalienable proofs.

The real problem is not a lack of evidence of God, but a willful heart that does not like what God says. "They did not like to retain God in their knowledge" (Romans 1:28). When we admit to ourselves that He is there, it follows that we are responsible to Him and to His words.

Faith and reason are great working partners. To believe in God, His book, and its message about the Savior is logic in action. Indeed, unbelief is unreasonable. For example, everyone accepts that an extraordinary result must have a corresponding cause, and no effect can be greater than its cause. The great inconsistency in unbelief is that it ignores that axiom. Unbelief is willing to accept great effects while denying a corresponding cause. The clock on the wall had to have an intelligent maker with a design. But unbelief looks at the infinitely greater clock of the universe, with its uncountable parts whirling through space in clock-like precision and draws a strange conclusion: It is the result of an indefinite explosion of something. Then the unbeliever goes and sets his own clock by it! If the desktop computer required a builder, surely the marvelously greater human brain did not make itself. If the television set required intelligence to build it, what of the complexity of sound and light waves that carry the picture and message across the world?

The avowed atheist (one who believes there is no god) is unreasonably proud and illogical. He contributes no good to our world. Can you think of any beneficial contributions he has made to society? Any colleges for the pursuit of truth? Any shelters for abused women? Any orphanages? Any havens for the homeless, aged, or handicapped? Ever see an atheistic hospital? We can give them credit for some things, like trying to run the Boy Scouts out of business, removing prayer from public schools, promoting an educational system devoid of morality, or costing us millions in frivolous lawsuits, including trying to remove "under God" from our pledge of allegiance and "in God we trust" from our currency. Atheists are such because they *will* to be. They do not *want* to believe in God.

The fact is you can have faith in God and Christ if you *will*. He invites us to believe because we can, if we will to believe.

Often faith is thought of as a means of getting something we want. But the function of faith is not to see what we can get but rather, to govern how we live. I read of a new man in town who drove around on Sunday morning trying to decide which church to attend. Finally he joined the church with all the Cadillacs and Lincolns in the parking lot. He said, "These folks must have a religion that works!"

It is a great mistake to think of church or of faith as something designed primarily to please us, or of God as a source for getting what we want – as if to say, "If I get Him on my side I can be successful, popular, or healthy." Jesus forewarned His followers to expect reverses and troubles. Peter advised us not to be surprised when fiery trials come our way. The promise to us is that when we pass through the deep waters, or the fire, He will be with us (Isaiah 43:2), as if to say, His followers *will* pass that way.

Faithful Christians may not be healthy or wealthy. Heroes of faith have been "destitute, afflicted, tormented" (Hebrews 11:37). But they continue to trust Him, knowing He is always with them, planning their eventual good. He is not a tool. He is the Master Craftsman.

True faith in God does not try to shape His word into the mold of the reader's bias or their own ideas. Let me illustrate with the actions of secular historians. People who write history or produce historical programs for television often create very different accounts of events, men, and movements. For instance, it is a historical fact that America had its roots with men of Christian faith. We have their writings and speeches to demonstrate that. But more recent historians, with bias against God, often delete such evidence from their histories, and thereby blot that element out of the record. Instead of striving for accurate portrayals of people who lived in those times, these prejudiced writers expose their beliefs that the educated opinions of the elite are more accurate than the actual facts of the case, though separated by centuries.

That is a common approach used in "interpreting" the Bible. On those pages are recorded statements and happenings that required the hand of God to interrupt the natural course of things such as Jonah and the whale, or Noah's flood, Jesus giving sight to the blind, raising the dead, et cetera. But unbelief does not like the idea of the miraculous, or of God intervening in human affairs. So they decide and insist that the writers did not mean what they wrote. Instead of accepting the eyewitness accounts of the contemporaries to the events (II Peter 1:16), they resort to calling such events allegories, untrue, or simple myths intended to teach something.

God's clear and plain truth is often so rejected because, if accepted, reason calls for personal action. Responsibility is laid on us. God is God. He is and must be sovereign, which demands the submission of faith.

True faith in God affects moral action. The manager of a certain business asked me to return his phone call. I did so within minutes. His secretary answered blithely, "Sorry, Mr. So and So is not in." When I protested that he had just asked me to call, there was a pause. Then she said, "Oh, perhaps he is in. Oh, yes, here he is." He was there all the time and she knew it, but for some reason, found it convenient to lie. Far from unusual, lying is practiced and excused all through our society. Promises are made with no intention of keeping them and not only by politicians. The merchant misrepresents his product. The attorney argues the innocence of the client he knows is guilty. A speaker exaggerates his story just to make himself look good. In fact, some people lie when it is easier to tell the truth. In some places, veracity and integrity are as scarce as a snake's hips.

Yes, people have the right to lie, but we who claim to have faith in God do not have that right. If we want a vibrant faith, we must turn away from sins that God so clearly forbids. We have the right to walk and act in any way we choose, but people will know the truth. Hypocrisy is so easily discovered.

When I asked, "Have you ever spoken audibly to God," the response was like so many others: "No." There was a hesitancy because God was somehow not as real as other persons. Faith was small. People are reluctant to talk to God – or about God – because their faith is weak. If God is discussed at all, He is referred to in such a fuzzy, obscure way as to make Him a non-entity. For example, speaking of God, "as you understand Him." Whatever God you imagine! Another speaker proclaims, "We come to God each in his own way." Some talk of "a higher power" in a completely ambiguous sense, without ever coming either to identify, or know Him, as though it were satisfactory faith to believe in such an obscure and variable god, moldable to any person's wishes. Such a god is not God at all.

Think about it. Could God be variable, subject to every person's fancy? If He is subject to a person's imagination, doesn't that make the person his own god? Is it really intelligent for a hundred people to believe in as many gods? He said, "I am the Lord, I change not," (Malachi 3:6). Is He not, then, absolute and unchanging? All of those fuzzy, nonsensical ideas about Him, which so many think to be a commendable faith, are really not true faith in God. Superstition manufactures a religion as a mask of respectability that permits us to live our own lifestyles, with no worry about pleasing the one true and holy God who will call every one of us into judgment.

He says, "I am the Lord and there is none else..." (Isaiah 45:5-6). "I ...am the Lord, and beside me there is no savior" (Isaiah

43:11). He is a person, the Creator, holy, just, and good. He will not overlook sin, but He loves sinners. He paid the sinners' debt. He defeated death. He offers the gift of everlasting life to all who will receive Him by faith.

Giving is a major theme of the Bible. God created the sun, moon, and stars "to give light..." (Genesis 1:17). Christ is coming again "...to give every man according as his work shall be" (Revelation 22:12). In between those first and last books of the Bible, we find the subject more than 2,000 times in statements like, "Who giveth us richly all things to enjoy?" (I Timothy 6:17). "Ask, and it shall be given you..." (Matthew 7:7).

The greatest gift ever given was when God gave His Son for you and me, and this lost, undeserving world. Greatest gift because it met our greatest need, at the greatest cost, revealing the greatest love, and with the greatest result God, Himself, could secure.

And He keeps on giving to those who accept His Gift. "He that spared not His own Son, but delivered Him up for us all, how shall He not with Him also freely give us all things?" (Romans 8:32).

But a gift is not a gift until it is accepted. The greatest of all tragedies is when a person rejects the Gift of God. He demonstrated the reality and validity of His offer of eternal life when Jesus rose from the dead. To refuse the Gift of God is to seal our own separation forever from the life He offers.

For many years, a young woman had been searching for the real meaning of life. Throughout adolescence, high school and college, then a successful professional career, there lingered this haunting curiosity: Where does the heart find true and lasting fulfillment? One day she met a friend who told her to read the Gospel of John. As she read the words, their meaning was obscure. Then she came to John 3. Verse 16 of that chapter is probably the best known sentence in the Bible. "For God so loved the world, that He gave His only begotten Son, that whosoever believeth in Him should not perish, but have everlasting life" (John 3:16).

She thought. Can it be that the great and high God in heaven loves me? That is what it says. I guess God can do whatever He wills, but would He take on Himself human flesh and come to this earth in the person of Jesus? That is what it says. And would such a one, out of love to me, die as my substitute? That is what it says. And can I have life, real life, and everlasting life by believing in Him? That is what it says.

Does it work? It did for her, for she did come to trust Christ and believe His Word. She found the answer, as have multitudes of others who have put their faith in Him, committing themselves to the Savior. "...We may know Him that is true; and we are in Him that is true, even in His Son Jesus Christ. This is the true God, and eternal life" (I John 5:20).

# CHAPTER 14

# REAL CHARISMA

I read a newspaper article about charismatic animals! I said to myself, "Whoa! What kind are those?" The word, charisma, is a Greek word from the Bible that has in recent years come into common use and is often misused. A politician, or other public figure may be said to have a charismatic personality, by which is meant, pleasing. A person may have "charisma." Often, churches and people who practice speaking in strange tongues are referred to as charismatics.

But such is not the accurate meaning of the word, charisma. It does not mean "tongues." Nor does it mean an outgoing, winsome personality. It means "gift" as in Romans 6:23: "...the *gift* of God is eternal life through Jesus Christ our Lord." Have you received the gift of God? When we consider what is in the gift and the wealth of the Giver, we get an idea of its inestimable value.

The related Greek word is "charis", which means grace, or loveliness. It appears in Ephesians 2:8, "For by *grace* are ye saved through faith," and we are challenged, "Let your speech be always with *grace*" (Colossians 4:6).

The wonderful grace of God (charis) provides the wonderful gift (charisma) of salvation and everlasting life in Jesus Christ, God's Son. When we receive God's gift, we participate in His grace, and the product is grace in life and conduct. That is true charisma.

One part of God's gift of salvation is the power and ability to have victory over sinful habits and attitudes. The promise is, "Sin shall not have dominion over you" (Romans 6:14). People crave many things, not all of them good. There are appetites that can threaten and destroy us. The desire for possessions can make us greedy, envious, and dishonest. An undisciplined hunger for food is not healthy for us (or for our dogs). An appetite for alcohol can ruin a body and soul for time and eternity (I Corinthians 6:10). The lust for tobacco has destroyed many. Sexual appetite, if uncontrolled, will undermine our sense of morality. If indulged, it will lead us to rationalize evil actions. The Bible pronounces woe for those who call evil, good, and good, evil, who put darkness for light, and light for darkness, (Isaiah 5:20). When we indulge such appetites, we are likely to get hooked by them, and then shift the blame of responsibility away from ourselves to the mystery power of some substance – or our genes.

There is a profound, wonderful, and simple cure for that out-of-control appetite. The answer is salvation in Christ.

> Christ is the answer to all our problems,
> He holds the key to the whole world's need.
> If you receive Him – if you believe Him,
> He is the answer to all your need.
> -Charles Wesley

"He breaks the power of canceled sin and sets the prisoner free." He is "the power of God and the wisdom of God" (I Corinthians 1:24). "I can do all things through Christ, who strengtheneth me" (Philippians 4:13).

Jesus Christ is our only hope of everlasting life (Acts 4:12). Jesus Christ is the one and only bridge from man to God (I Timothy 2:5). Jesus Christ alone is the sure, unfailing remedy for victory over those destructive appetites and sins of the flesh. He can meet our need because of who He is.

People have different responses to the question, "What about God and your relationship to Him?" One man responded, "I never think about those things." All his thinking was taken up with his work, money, and fun. I knew his answer was not altogether true, for it is in man's nature to sometimes wonder about God and what lies beyond.

Another response came from a hospital patient who had a needle in her arm, dripping caustic chemicals into her system in an attempt to ward off the dreaded cancer. She bristled in great anger at the very mention of God – whom she would likely meet soon!

Yet another replied, "If I ever did get interested in religion, how could I ever know which one is right?" Good question. The field has become such a confusing maze that some are tempted to give up on finding the truth of God.

Here are some clues:

1. Who in the field defeated death and rose from the grave? Interesting that there is only one who makes that claim. He must know something about immortality. Pick the winner; why follow a loser?
2. What religious message has so profoundly affected the world, being tried and proven by millions whose lives have been changed for good?
3. What religion is so opposed by the anti-God crowd? Bible-believing Christians are derisively ridiculed as extremists. If you believed the ACLU, you would think Christians are America's worst enemies.
4. Next time you go to church, look around and ask yourself how many are holding a Bible – and does the speaker use it honestly.

Jesus said, "If any man will do His will, he shall know of the doctrine..." (John 7:17).

If there is darkness, there has to be light.

If there is falsehood, there has to be truth.

If there is confusion, there has be order by which to gauge it.

In religion, where there is confusion, it is because an enemy of truth is trying to keep souls in the dark.

Alaskans love to go fishing. Halibut, king salmon, trout, grayling, crabs, clams – Alaskans love to go for all of them. Seems like nearly everybody enjoys goin' fishin'. And God has surely blessed this country with bounty.

It is interesting that when the Son of God chose special men to be His disciples, the majority were either commercial fishermen, or just "went fishin'." His words to them were, "Follow me, and I will make you fishers of men" (Matthew 4:19).

That suggests, first, that men have such great value to God that He desires to "catch" us. Though we may well wonder how that could possibly be, it is the major message of the Bible. "God so loved the world that He gave His only begotten Son..." (John 3:16). A simple statement, yet none is so profound. God loves you! Try saying, "God loves me!"

Second, men and women need "catching." Unless He catches them, they will not realize their full potential in time or eternity. Until one is brought home in God's net, he is lost and life is empty. Questions without answers. A maze with no exit. But the God of love would catch you with the gospel of saving Grace, give you life abundantly, and shepherd you. His invitation is, "Come unto me, all ye that labor and are heavy laden, and I will give you rest" (Matthew 11:28).

# CHAPTER 15

# REAL HAPPINESS

"How can I feel good about myself" is a question often asked. Books, articles, advertisements, television programs all offer advice. The psychologist thinks he knows and is happy to give counsel – for a price. You can buy a wig to cover your bald head, pay a surgeon for a face lift, or remove your stomach to make you thin.

> Mirror; mirror on the dresser,
> Don't I look a little lesser?

We are counseled to get college degrees, wear the right clothes, control habits, project successful images, and drink only diet sodas. But have you met people who have done some or all of the above, and, yet, they are unhappy?

No doubt we are overly obsessed with number one, making the big "I" happy. It is strange but true that the condition of happiness is not found by focusing on making ourselves happy. We can be proud of ourselves and lose happiness. Bible advice is the best advice and we are instructed there to stop that drive to please self, and develop an interest in the lives and well-being of others.

Here is where that road begins: "Blessed are the poor in spirit, for theirs is the kingdom of heaven" (Matthew 5:3). The word, "blessed" means happy and fulfilled. It is not "blessed are the rich, the beautiful, the proud," but "the poor in spirit." That has nothing to do with money. Nor is it the same as weak-spirited. David in the Bible was poor in spirit, but also strong-spirited.

Poor in spirit, simply put, means I have no spiritual assets. I need everything in that department. So I take my place in the dust before a holy God. I acknowledge my spiritual poverty and gladly receive His gifts of salvation and life in Christ. That is the greatest of all treasures, and when we have it, we have happiness.

There is not a single "blessed" in the Bible for having anything else, or for doing something. What we are in heart and soul is everything. Our world supposes that comfort, gratification, and convenience equal contentment, but with time and experience we learn that it is all vanity, unable to satisfy the heart. If we believed many of our sociologists, politicians, and news editors, we would think that if we had our pockets full of money and never got sick, we would be contented.

Consider good health. It is wonderful. We have found that exercise promotes good health, contributing to a sense of well-being. The Bible seems to agree. Back in the days when people walked everywhere, often hundreds of miles, Paul wrote to Timothy that there is some value in physical exercise (I Timothy 4:8). We note, however, that young, healthy people still commit suicide. Unhappy. It is a strange set of values that causes many to spend so much energy, money, and interest on a dying, physical body (it starts to die as soon as we are born!) while they invest nothing on the real self, that is, the soul that outlives the body. They spend thousands of dollars on insurance, but are careless about insuring the soul.

Consider those who are financially prosperous. Why do so many of them commit suicide? A suitcase full of money cannot bring contentment. The news reports on people with astronomical annual incomes, who never have enough, stooping to fraud to satisfy their greed. Are they contented?

Ours is a day of constant, unrelenting advertising for an ever-increasing collection of gadgets, creature comforts, and toys for all ages. And it is all designed to make us discontented until we have this and that. Consequently, the rarest commodity on the market is contentment. There is even that widespread rumor, often pushed by the television evangelist, that financial prosperity and physical health indicate spiritual health and that God's approval rests on the affluent lifestyle. Wrong! Some believe that poor health and low income indicate God's disfavor. Wrong again.

Often God's choice servants have lived and died in what the world calls poverty or poor health – contented! The Apostle Paul, faithful and fruitful servant of God, had physical problems and was martyred, penniless, in a Roman dungeon. He wrote, "I have learned, in whatever state I am, in this to be content" (Philippians 4:11). The people of God find contentment under any and all circumstances. Several Bible statements give the divine doctor's prescription for it. "Godliness with contentment is great gain" (I Timothy 6:6). Material gain neither produces nor proves godliness. But godliness in Christ is great gain. "Let your manner of life be without covetousness, and be content with such things as ye have; for He hath said, I will never leave thee nor forsake thee" (Hebrews 13:5).

> Had I wealth and love in fullest measure,
> And a name revered both far and near,
> Yet no hope beyond, no harbor waiting,
> Where my storm tossed vessel I could steer;
> If I gained the world, but lost the Savior,
> Who endured the cross, and died for me,
> Could then all the world afford a refuge,
> Whither in my anguish, I might flee?
>
> -Anna Olander

Have you come to the living Christ? In trusting Him you "find" God and you find contentment.

There are also some negatives – some things we are cautioned against doing if we would find happiness.

1. Blessed (happy) is the one who is not guided by the wisdom of ungodly people. "Blessed is the man who walketh not in the counsel of the ungodly" (Psalm 1:1). Do not get your philosophy of life from those who only

know life apart from their Creator. One of them might say, "Live life fast and merry" or, "Do your own thing" or, "Get rich and die rich." They may fool others for awhile, but they live and die unhappy. All the glitz, noise, and activity cannot cover the reality of emptiness.

2. Happy is the one who avoids the company of sinful people: "...nor standeth in the way of sinners" (Psalm 1:1). He does not walk with those who do wrong. He recognizes the sinful lifestyle and its pitfalls, and he will not walk or stand there, regardless of peer pressure.

3. Happy is the one who will not keep company with scornful people: "...nor sitteth in the seat of the scornful" (Psalm 1:1). There are plenty of ungodly people who ridicule and scoff at God and God's people, crude jokes – that good people neither laugh at nor listen to. "Evil company corrupts good morals" (I Corinthians 15:33).

4. In Psalm 1, verse 2, the happy person delights in God's laws. He cultivates a taste for godliness and a desire to do His will and please Him. They "hunger and thirst after righteousness" (Matthew 5:6).

Do not expect that God will do for you that which He has told you to do for yourself. And He does not give His help to those who are half-hearted, holding a low value for spiritual things. His gift of eternal life is not for those who are careless about it. Those who are indifferent or negligent of duty do not know his power for victory and success in Christian living. To grow in grace requires diligence.

Christian maturity, knowledge of God's presence, victory over sins of the flesh, the ability to help others, vibrant faith and prayer – these do not just happen. They are not in some people's genes. Nor does God give them automatically to a privileged few. They grow out of the discipline of obedience and following the Good Shepherd. We are challenged to "grow in grace" (II Peter 3:18), as though it was our responsibility. "Give all diligence, add to your faith" (II Peter 1:5). "Run with patience the race that is set before us" (Hebrews 12:1). "Put on the whole armor of God, that ye may be able to stand" (Ephesians 6:11). Then that armor is catalogued, so we can know what we are to put on. Mother must dress the toddler, but when he grows up, he dresses himself.

# CHAPTER 16

# REAL SERVING

C hristian victory and maturity require work and effort on our part. Wonderful provision is made for us in the person of the Holy Spirit, but He expects our partnership. There is a cost of victory. Salvation is free. Discipleship is costly. The prize is for the winner.

Serving is vital to maturing. There has to be an outlet for that which we take in. Standing water stagnates. Fill the glass with milk, and if unused, it sours. It is the same with us. We can take in the teaching of the Word, enjoy the preacher, attend all the meetings, memorize the songs and read the Bible, but unless we learn and practice some way of using all of that, we remain immature and liable to sour. The Lord, of course, knew that when He said, "Ye shall receive power, after that the Holy Spirit is come upon you; and ye shall be witnesses unto me…" (Acts 1:8). Note there, that the Holy Spirit was not given to simply make us feel good, but to empower us to serve.

Ours is a consumer-oriented society. Advertisers, shopping malls, restaurants, travel agencies, car salesmen, et cetera all aim at pleasing the consumer, who is constantly reminded that he owes himself all these goodies, and ought to have them all, or he will never enjoy the "good life." Through all of it, we have developed a mind-set that expects to be catered to. There are many "consumer Christians" who have adopted that philosophy. They pick a church on the principle of what it will do for them, rather than on its scriptural position, doctrinal truth, and an opportunity to serve. Church attendance becomes a spectator sport and pastors are glad to accommodate such with an entertainment gospel. I suggest that if we are serious about finding the best Christ has to offer, that we "renew [our] mind" (Romans 12:2), give our "bodies a living sacrifice" (Romans 12:1), stop expecting to be catered to, and get involved in some effort demanding service for the King. It is amazing how quickly we learn to love the church, its warmth, and its fellowship, which we may have previously missed when we did not serve.

Why go to church anyway? "You don't need to go to church to be a Christian." Are you sure about that? "I can worship God out in the wilderness." I suppose so, but who or what do you really worship there? Too many of us have a cavalier, take it or leave it attitude about church. Two or three shots a year are enough. If we miss more than we attend, it is no big deal. "What church do you attend?" "Oh, I go to First Whatever." "Who is the pastor there?" "Ah, let me ask my wife."

Look what God says about it: "Forsake not the assembling of yourselves together" (Hebrews 10:25). Motivate one another "to love and to good works" (Hebrews 10:24).

The church is where you find qualified, and God-appointed teachers and pastors to aid you in the development of Christian maturity. We all need to avail ourselves of that opportunity (Ephesians 4:11-14). The church is the organism, which the Lord Jesus himself is building (Matthew 16:18). The church is where you are most likely to find the Lord (Revelation 1:13, 20, Matthew 18:20). The church is where the Lord's supper is observed to remind us of Him (Luke 22:19-20) The church is the pillar and ground of the truth (I Timothy 3:15).

Suppose everybody was indifferent about the church and neglected to be involved. Soon there would be no churches. Do we want a city or a nation absent the moral standards and righteousness promoted exclusively by Bible-believing churches?

One reason the Lord calls His followers sheep (Psalm 23, John 10) is because of our gregarious, sociable nature. We are not called grizzly bears. We need each other. The church is His provision for that. Church involvement is the right thing to do if we are serious about God's revealed will.

Ready mix. From concrete to financial planning, we buy TV dinners, salad, hot potatoes, chicken – everything all ready for the palate. Do not make me fix it. Just let me consume it. Convenient and quick.

Many "worshipers" carry the same system into church. Make it as easy for me (and quick) as you can. Do not ask me to put out any effort. Entertain me. Please me; you cook up the menu, set the table, and serve me. If I like the menu and atmosphere, I will come and eat but if I do not like your fixins', next week I will try another restaurant.

How about putting the whole church service on video or maybe an overhead projector? Then the performers, including the preacher, could produce commercial grade services. Take the old hymnbook out of the pews; we wont need it. It was too old fashioned anyway. We could put the whole Bible text on the overhead too, so worshipers would not have to carry their Bibles, or be bothered with looking for the text.

We are producing formula-fed, spiritually lazy "Christians" who never exercise any disciplined effort to study the Word of God that does not change with the times, but "liveth and abideth forever" (I Peter 1:23). We get out of anything according to what we put in. What makes a Christian church dead or alive for us is, to a high degree, our commitment to the Head of the Church, Jesus Christ.

We admire the nobility of those who search (or examine) the scriptures (Acts 17:11). It is our natural tendency to weaken toward decay. Strong buildings require labor and maintenance. The Church of Jesus Christ is called the "house of God" (I Timothy 3:15). It deserves our effort. Mediocrity is a blight on popular Christianity. Put some effort into the cooking; follow the right recipe (The Bible), and we will be far more satisfied with the meal – forever.

Often I have heard a well-meaning parent say, "I will not make my kids go to church, but when they get older, they can choose for themselves". Strange that they do not follow that reasoning in other areas of their child's life. I have seen kids hoot and holler because they did not want to go to kindergarten or first grade. But a wise and loving parent knows what is good for them, so they give them no choice; they make them go to school. I do not remember a dad or a mom say "I do not care if he takes a bath or not. I will wait until he gets older and let him choose for himself". No, a wise parent understands the need of steering and training for the benefit of the child he loves.

Consider these benefits for children in a good church. They learn how to sit quietly, how to control themselves. It may take a few weeks, but it is an important lesson, well worth the effort. They learn how to interact with other kids and adults, and make friends with good kids. They learn how to sing wholesome songs and how to express themselves. They learn how to concentrate and think. They learn how to distinguish between things that are good and things that are not good. They learn reverence for the greatest book ever written. They are exposed to the important spiritual side of life that is so carefully avoided in the public schools.

What is bad about all of that? Surely those things are important to developing the kind of lives parents will be happy about.

Some parents are greatly involved in the lives of their children, running daily to something or other – music lessons, swimming, hockey, baseball, basketball, soccer, football, et cetera. Good activities and commendable parental interest. But what are the priorities? Is anything more important than truth, morality, and a good relationship to God?

Rather than making your kids go to church, *take* them. It will pay great dividends for both of you.

One day a soldier out on the battlefield was commanded to guard and keep an important prisoner. If he escaped, the soldier would have to take the prisoner's place, or be fined a large sum of money. Well, when the officer returned, the prisoner had escaped. The guard's excuse was, "While I was busy here and there, he was gone" (I Kings 20:40), which was no excuse at all.

Busy! That is life. Somebody said he was busy "clear into the middle of next month!" We are all pressured with business, house care, family care, taxes, school, vacations, and just keeping ahead of the weather. Everyone has the same amount of time – 24 hours a day to get it all in. Always short of time, everybody has a life full of more than they will ever get done. Challenging, is it not?

Probably the most common excuses a preacher hears are, "Well, I'm just too busy. I don't have time to attend church," "Sunday is my only day off." No time for God, my Maker and Judge – and so we fail to meet the one major responsibility in life, the keeping of our never dying soul. Benjamin Franklin said, "The man who is good for excuses is good for nothing else." So, your Superior comes, you look around you, and everything is gone. Time, health, money, opportunity – and your soul. All gone forever.

When that soldier excused his neglect of responsibility to his commander with, "I was busy,: he threw away any good reason he might have had. For if he was busy about other things here and there, he could have given attention to the prisoner, had he wanted to. That is it. The commanding officer was less important than things here and there.

# CHAPTER 17

# REAL CHRISTIAN

When the Lord Jesus walked here, they asked Him, "What is the first and greatest commandment?" He answered, "Thou shalt love the Lord, thy God, with all thy heart, and with all thy soul, and with all thy mind" (Matthew 22:37). Do you love God? I am not asking do you know about God, or even do you believe in God, but do you *love* God? The question should not make you uncomfortable. It is not meant to be confrontational, but invitational.

The preacher is sometimes dismissed with the umbrella statement, "I am a Christian." The claimant may not attend church, as true Christians do (Hebrews 10:25). He usually feels that because he is good to others, he will go to heaven, even though the Bible clearly teaches that our good works cannot save us. He may not even believe that Christ was God come in human flesh. Jesus said, "If ye believe not that I am He, ye shall die in your sins" (John 8:24). One cannot be a Christian and reject Christ.

Our ideas and opinions about Christ have become so mixed and blended that for some, it is hard to define Biblical Christianity. Things clearly stated in Scripture are rejected and things clearly condemned there are accepted, promoted, and defended by some who insist that they are Christians.

If you count yourself to be a Christian, then you must love God, the first of all the commanded requirements. So, do you love God? Here is an easy test.

1. Do you think much of God? When we love someone or something, we think about it. "Where your treasure is, there will your heart be also" (Luke 12:34). Is God in your thoughts? Or do your think more about your investments, politics, or sports?

2. Do you desire to be near Him? People who love each other enjoy one another's company, talk to each other, and miss each other if long separated. He speaks in His Word. He dwells in His church. Do you meet Him there? "...He that loveth not his brother, whom he hath seen, how can he love God whom he hath not seen?" (I John 4:20).

3. Are you sensitive to that which displeases or dishonors Him? The sins of Sodom were a grief to Lot who was "...vexed with the filthy conversation of the wicked" (II Peter 2:7). Does it offend you when God and Christ are dishonored?

4. Do you love what God loves? David loved the words of, and the house of God. Is the day of worship of special value to you? Do you view it as an opportunity to be with Him and His family?

5. Do you want to be in heaven forever with Him? I am sure you do. Better come to love and obey heaven's King.

# CHAPTER 18

# REAL LIVING

The advertisement said, "Stop Aging Now! – Stop Getting Old!" Just take this little pill and stop getting old. I have not seen the statistics, but it is probably a safe bet that old age is our number one killer.

One old duffer said, "Don't die until you reach 100. Your chances will be better then, because few people die after 100."

If old age is our number one killer, then maybe, if we could keep from getting old, we might live forever. Pretty slim chance! There is a much more certain solution to the problem of dying. Many years ago one perfect Man came back from the dead. He told us the way to win over death. He said, "I give unto them eternal life; and they shall never perish" (John 10:28). Jesus Christ is the secret. He has life to give. "As the Father hath life in Himself, so hath He given to the Son to have life in Himself" (John 5:26).

Eternal life. It is the free gift to those who believe in Jesus. "And this is life eternal, that they might know thee, the only true God, and Jesus Christ, whom thou hast sent" (John 17:3). We read of a land that is fairer than day, a land where we will never grow old, a land where all our tears have been wiped away, and sorrow and sighing are no more. There is no night there, no sickness, no dying. No fighting or warfare, but peace forever. Heaven is a real and a wonderful place, beautiful beyond description. The Lord Jesus purchased a home there for us with His own blood. His promise is "He that hears my word, and believes on Him that sent me, hath everlasting life, and shall not come into judgment, but is passed from death into life" (John 5:24).

There is far more to life than the material or physical. There is that which the material or physical can never satisfy. There is the spiritual reality. There is a soul. It cannot be seen. It does not show on an MRI, but the doctor can tell when it departs. Obviously, many people focus on building bodies and bank accounts and leave the spiritual part to shrivel like a dried bean. The trouble is, that which is inside of us is the only part of us that lives on. Bodies ruin, and money rots, but the real self goes on living in heaven or hell.

We are driven and act in accordance with beliefs and ideas. Pragmatism is the doctrine that results are the sole test of the validity of one's ideas or beliefs. It asks, "What will this do for me?" It does not weigh a belief in the scale of truth, but weighs it with a question, "What is in it for me?"

Another doctrine is materialism. It postulates that physical laws can explain everything in the universe. Material and physical well-being make up the highest good. The materialist is interested only in the physical aspects of life, like bodies, money, and items that money can buy. Talk to him of spiritual matters, or the life to come, and he dismisses the subject – or ridicules it as pie in the sky by and by.

The consequence is that you never get to the heart of either personal or social problems. We are rightly concerned about destructive moral trends in society, but most of the suggested remedies are physical and material. Throw more money at the problem; tax the problem; educate about the results of the problem; tighten the laws, et cetera, but never address the spiritual root. When will we come to understand that those outer actions and lifestyle result from the unseeable inside? "Out of [the heart] are the issues of life" (Proverbs 4:23). "As [a man[ thinks in his heart, so is he" (Proverbs 23:7).

What could possibly be more practical than to be made spiritually alive, by the experience of the new and spiritual birth with the result of lasting inner peace, an abundant life, and the solid, positive assurance of everlasting life?

## CHAPTER 19

# REAL SECURITY

I was trying to interest a young, self-confident engineer in God's offer of salvation. I asked him if he had an answer for those three philosophical questions that so often trouble and nag at people. "Where did I come from?" "Why am I here?" "Where am I going?"

"Oh," he answered, "those things do not bother me at all! Where did I come from? I do not care! I am just here. Why am I here? Just to live and enjoy myself! Where am I going? Nowhere! When it is over, it is over and there is nothing beyond!"

All those answers may be neat, but very thoughtless. If we live with that philosophy for a while, we will discover its emptiness giving neither peace nor security. However, there was no use to argue with that young, self-assured man, so I asked "Why is it that people cannot get along with each other, or their own selves while we are here? Why is this world full of hatred, division, fighting, bloodshed, and suicide, especially when there are so many good reasons why we ought to have peace with each other?"

"Well," he said, "that is the only question that bothers me."

Of course, there is no answer other than that given in the Bible – the sin problem.

How wonderfully reasonable and believable is God's Word. It answers all our questions. There is a sovereign, all-wise God who made us. Satan and sin entered and messed up what God created. So, while 21st century mankind bears the evidence of the special handiwork of God, we also constantly bear the evidence of sin's ruinous effects. So we struggle. But that great God still loves people, so He designed and carried out a marvelous plan of redemption. His eternal, sinless Son came here to live and die as our substitute, pay the sin debt we owed, satisfy the demands of perfect justice, and then to rise from the dead to make everlasting life available to all who identify with Him and receive Him by faith.

Where did I come from? God the Creator! Why am I here? To live for and please Him. Where am I going? To the heaven God has prepared for those who love Him, secure forever!

# CHAPTER 20

# REAL PEACE

W hen Jesus was born in Bethlehem, angels announced His
birth with a promise, "On earth, peace, good will toward
men" (Luke 2:14). He is called the Prince of Peace. The night
before He was crucified, He said, "Peace I leave with you, my
peace I give unto you" (John 14:27). Nineteen of the 27 books of
the New Testament begin with "peace be to you." Now, 20 centuries
later, we live in a war-torn and troubled world with its multitudes
that are strangers to peace. Is the Bible promise all hollow idealism
without substance? Did Jesus Christ fail in His mission? Where is
the peace He was to bring?

Consider these three facts:

1. There can be no universal peace in a world at odds with
   our Creator. From His perspective, the whole world lies
   in wickedness (I John 5:19).
2. There is coming, and just ahead of us, a real new age
   when Jesus Christ fulfills His promise to come to this
   world again. Then He will clean house and establish a
   worldwide kingdom over which He will reign in perfect
   righteousness, establishing and maintaining peace
   (Isaiah 2:4).
3. Wonderful and lasting personal peace is attainable, to be
   experienced today – now. Christ paid for our redemption,

reconciling us to God, and "made peace through the blood of His cross" (Colossians 1:20). Now, risen from the dead, He invites us to be reconciled to God by receiving Him in faith.

Peace with God must come first. Then peace with ourselves, and peace with others. Peace, despite any storm. How do we explain it? It "passeth all understanding" (Philippians 4:7). What does it cover? "Your hearts and minds." That is, your emotions and intellect. How do we experience it for our own? "Being justified by faith, we have peace with God through our Lord Jesus Christ." (Romans 5:1). True Christianity means pardon for sin, heaven forever, and perfect peace today. "Thou wilt keep him in perfect peace, whose mind is stayed on thee, because he trusteth in thee" (Isaiah 26:3).

For those who have tested and proved its reality, it is hard to imagine anyone rejecting it. Why is this, that the One best qualified to help is so often the last one we go to for help?

A young woman with a load of family problems came seeking financial help. At the simple mention of God, she stormed out in anger. Another runs into my car at an intersection, is upset and crying, but when I suggest that there is One who cares and comforts, she explodes in bitter resentment. The cancer victim, or that one in declining days, closes the door on a friendly conversation with a blunt, "I do not want to talk about that."

Indeed strange it is to throw away the best hope of help when help is so desperately needed. Is it pride? Is it a prejudice against "religion" that has been nourished over the years? Is it awareness that if we have a relationship with God, He would correct some things? Can it be that God is bad for us? We enter this world with an empty bank account, and we go out the same way unless we receive God's gift. "We brought nothing into this world, and it is certain we can carry nothing out" (I Timothy 6:7). If along the way we "find" Him, we are rich forever.

A safe, reliable boat needs a good compass to keep it on course over the distance. It needs a rudder to steer it on the right heading. It needs a power source to propel it in the right direction. It needs an anchor to put down in the storm. It needs a capable Captain to coordinate all the above, to intelligently carry it across the waters to the desired harbor.

We are like that boat. We need a reliable compass. That is why we need the Bible. Use it and refer to it often. "Thy Word is a lamp unto my feet, and a light unto my path" (Psalm 119:105).

We need a power source for our voyage. That is why we need the new birth (John 3) and the power of the Holy Spirit that comes with that new birth.

We need a rudder to keep us on the right course. That is why the Lord promised to dwell with us personally and never leave us. "For He hath said, I will never leave thee, nor forsake thee" (Hebrews 13:5b).

We need an anchor for the storms of life. That is why God gave to us His promises, which cannot fail. "Which hope we have as an anchor of the soul, both sure and steadfast, and which entereth into that within the veil" (Hebrews 6:19).

> We have an anchor that keeps the soul,
> Steadfast and sure while the billows roll;
> Fastened to the rock which cannot move,
> Grounded firm and deep in the Savior's love.
>                                         -Priscilla J. Owens

And we need the Good Captain to coordinate everything, keep us, and direct us. A million and more have given Him the command of the Ship of Life and made Him the Captain of their salvation. Or, to change the metaphor, have made Him the Shepherd of Life, proving that He leads besides still waters, satisfies completely, and leads to safe harbor. He can be depended on!

# CHAPTER 21

# THE REAL WAY

It is supremely important to understand that Jesus Christ is the only and the all-sufficient way to peace with God. He is "the author and finisher of our faith" (Hebrews 12:2). He is "The Alpha and Omega" (Revelation 1:8). He is the subject, the object, and everything in between, the all in all of our salvation. This needs emphasis because so many want to add some good that they have done, or can do, to the recipe. It is commendable and right to do well. Generosity, kindness, peace-making, faithfulness, and so on are right things to do, but we cannot depend on them to pay our sin debt and earn peace with God. Church attendance, if it is a Bible-based church, is good. But that of itself is not salvation. Carefully celebrating and observing religious rituals and ceremonies does not profit us to earn God's favor and salvation.

Several Bible statements are used to try to prove that we must be baptized to be saved. One is found in Mark 16:16, "He that believeth and is baptized shall be saved; but he that believeth not shall be damned." Please note it does not say there, or anywhere, that he who is not baptized shall be damned. The requirement for salvation is always belief in Christ. He pronounced a woman saved with the words, "Thy sins are forgiven" (Luke 7:48). She had not been baptized. The believing thief on the cross had not been baptized, yet Jesus said to him, "Today shalt thou be with me in paradise" (Luke 23:43).

Another statement often used to prove the need of baptism for salvation is that of Peter, "Repent, and be baptized, every one of you, in the name of Jesus Christ for the remission of sins…" (Acts 2:38). The key word there, relating to our subject, is the word "for." It is an indefinite preposition of reference (Greek, eis). In Acts 2:25 the same word is translated, "concerning." If Peter's instructions there taught that baptism was necessary as a means of salvation, it would be a contradiction of every formula for salvation given in the Bible. Of course, the Bible cannot contradict itself. The Greek word "for" can have a variety of meanings, as is true also in English. It may not mean "in order to" but often means "on the grounds of" or "on the basis of." We can be arrested for speeding, meaning not in order to speed, but because we were speeding. So baptism, according to Peter, was to be observed as a result of, or on the grounds of salvation and the remission of sins.

Yet another statement, also by Peter, is sometimes used to press regeneration through the rite of baptism. "The like figure unto which even baptism doth also now save us [not the putting away of the filth of the flesh, but the answer of a good conscience toward God], by the resurrection of Jesus Christ" (I Peter 3:21). It says that baptism is a figure like Noah and the flood. The preceding verse states that Noah and his family were saved by water. Clearly the floodwaters did not save Noah, and Peter did not mean that. The waters came as God's judgment of sin. The ark carried them above the waters. The ark is a type of Christ who is our refuge and safety. Biblical water baptism is a public testimony to the fact that we have by faith come into that ark for safety. The believer goes beneath the water, picturing his identification with the death of Christ for sin, paying its judgment. Then, coming up out of the water, he pictures his identification with Jesus to new life. So Peter there calls baptism a "figure," a picture of what we have done in accepting Christ. Then he says explicitly "not the putting away of the filth of the flesh." It has no earning merit to forgive sins. But its value lies in the "answer of a good conscience," that he is obedient in the matter of baptism and testimony.

The grand formula for being reconciled to God and finding the peace He gives is always the same. And, though profound, yet it is simple enough that even little children can understand. "Believe on the Lord Jesus Christ, and thou shalt be saved…" (Acts 16:31). Jesus paid it all. Nothing remains to be done, or added. By simply believing in Jesus, putting our faith in Him, we have peace with God.

One spoke of the "Venture of Faith." I would suggest the *Ad*venture of Faith. The word "venture" carries some baggage of risk, or chance, or speculation. Faith in Christ carries no risk whatsoever.

Now, flying is a venture. Alaska without airplanes would not be the Alaska we know. Every day thousands strap themselves into flying machines and take off for distant places with little thought of danger. Remember your first flight? There was that mixture of challenge, excitement, and phobia. You hated height, but then you fell in love with it (or did you?) and said to yourself, "What a wonderful scene is the flying machine!" So, now you join a couple of hundred crazies and climb confidently aboard that contraption to fly away up there with the clouds. Just one step could plunge you to a thousand deaths, yet you cruise merrily along with complete trust in machinery, and mechanics, and engineers, and pilots who are total strangers. One small malfunction anywhere along the line would be enough to stop your heart. Flying is a venture.

Heidi was to be a counselor at our summer camp. She had just disembarked from a jet, fresh to Alaska from a college "Outside." My job was to meet her and fly her on down to the Kenai, and our camp. As we collected her baggage and headed for the Piper Cub, I asked, "Have you ever ridden in a small airplane?" She answered quietly with a polite, "No," blissfully ignorant of what was ahead. As we pulled up to the cub, she exclaimed with obvious concern, "Wow! This is a small airplane!" So I spent several minutes explaining how it works and that it is really quite safe, trying to subdue her fears. She soon became a happy and pleasant passenger. Flying airplanes is a venture – Boeing 747 or Piper Cub. Faith in Christ is no risk, but always an *ad*venture.

How is it that so many take no thought and make no preparation for the greatest flight? We merrily head for that final airport where each of us must go through the "departure gate" without a thought of our destination, which "gate" we enter, and very little concern for the airship that will carry us somewhere, forever. There is no return flight. If we go through the wrong gate, get on the wrong flight, there will be a terrible wreck at the termination. But if we enter the narrow gate, and the right flight with the Lord as Captain, we are guaranteed safe arrival in a home called Heaven – and with excellent service all the way there.

If you do not yet have your ticket, come; there are still seats available. Jesus said, "I am the way, the truth, and the life; no man cometh unto the Father, but by me" (John 14:6). Surrender to Him. Trust Him. Put your faith in the Son of God and what He has done for you. No risk there but each day is a great adventure. "Then thou shalt understand the fear of the Lord, and find the knowledge of God" (Proverbs 2:5).